Learning Centers II

PRACTICAL IDEAS FOR YOU

Louise F. Waynant
Prince George's County, Maryland
Board of Education

Instructo/McGraw-Hill
Paoli, Pennsylvania 19301

Editorial Staff: *Research and Development Department Instructo / McGraw-Hill*

Cover Design: *Sam Ciccone*

Illustrations: *Carole Smith*

ACKNOWLEDGEMENTS

The author gratefully acknowledges the assistance and suggestions provided by *Ms. Bonnie Baden, Ms. Lynn Green, Ms. Barbara Kapinus, Ms. Priscella Pilson, and Ms. Marcia Waynant.*

The author is deeply indebted to *Dr. J. Richard Lewis* for his recommendations and encouragement.

The author extends her affection and gratitude to *Ms. Pat Richards* for her invaluable assistance, direction, and encouragement throughout this project.

DEDICATION

For my parents, with love.

10 9 8 7 6 5

Library of Congress Cataloging in Publication Data

Waynant, Louise F
   Learning centers ... practical ideas for you.

   Includes index.
   1. Instructional materials centers. I. Title.
LB3044.W39   371.3'078   76-44393
ISBN 0-07-082048-1

Table of Contents

Developing and Using Learning Centers

What Are Learning Centers?

Learning centers are sets of student-directed activities developed on the basis of specific objectives. Centers may be designed to introduce, develop, and reinforce skills or concepts. In addition, centers may be designed to provide diagnostic information and to develop or extend interests.

What Are the Characteristics of Learning Centers?

Learning centers usually have several of the following characteristics:

a. Clearly stated objectives

Objectives state what students will accomplish at the center. The objectives for every center should be written on the center. They should be written in terms that students can read and understand. Objectives should help students know what they are to learn, understand why they are doing the activities in a learning center, and assist students to determine if they have adequately accomplished the tasks in the center.

b. Clear directions

Center directions should enable students to work independently and determine when tasks have been completed.

c. Multi-level activities

Activities representing various levels of difficulty provide opportunities for individual student growth within a center. Furthermore, these activities enable students with different skill strengths to use the center activities.

d. Feedback system

Students need to know if they have responded correctly, if they have reached the objectives for which the center has been developed, and if they need further work with the skills or concepts presented in the center. Whenever possible, non open-ended center activities should be self-correcting so students may obtain immediate feedback. Other strategies for providing feedback in addition to self-correction are self-evaluation (how students feel about the task accomplished), teacher correction, informal teacher observation, and student-teacher conferences.

e. Manipulative devices

Whenever possible, centers should include manipulative devices which increase student involvement, interest, and motivation. Examples of manipulative devices include puzzles, pocket cards or charts, sets of cards used for matching and categorizing, spinner activities, and learning cubes.

How Are Learning Centers Developed?

When developing a center, the first step is to determine the purpose for the center. Will the center introduce, develop, or reinforce concepts or skills? Will it extend students' interests? Will it be used to provide diagnostic information?

After the purpose for the center has been established, specific objectives for the center should be defined. These objectives should be expressed in terms which students can understand, and written directly on the center. (E.g., "You (Students) will identify statements of fact and statements of opinion.")

A third step in center development is to plan the activities which students will perform in order to reach the center objectives. Activities might involve having students receive information (e.g., reading, listening, observing, examining), express information (e.g., writing, discussing, explaining, illustrating) or a combination of the two (e.g., experimenting, contrasting, describing, comparing).

Both open-ended activities and non open-ended activities might be included in the center. Open-ended activities often provide more opportunities for critical and creative thinking than those which are not open-ended. Several techniques for self-correction can be used with non open-ended activities. Among these techniques are separate answer keys; color, number, letter, or picture coding; puzzle formats, and covered answers.

When appropriate activities have been identified, they should be ordered according to their level of difficulty. Among the factors which affect the difficulty level of center activities are the quantity of material to be completed, the complexity of tasks involved, the amount of new information included, the amount of assistance available to the students, the amount and difficulty level of reading required to accomplish center tasks, and the extent to which tasks involve recall (rather than recognition) of information.

A fourth step in developing centers is to collect materials and construct or assemble the activities. To make the most efficient use of time and materials, it first should be determined if appropriate commercial (published) materials are available which might be used or adapted for use in the center activities. If center activities must be constructed, parts of these activities may be made more durable by laminating them, covering them with clear contact paper, mounting them, or enclosing them in acetate covers. Assistance in constructing the activities can be obtained from students, paraprofessionals, and volunteer parents.

A fifth step in center development is preparing directions for the center. Directions should be clear and legible, and should contain terminology familiar to students. Use of audio-visual aids such as tapes, illustrations, and photographs can assist students to follow directions independently. Another strategy which is helpful to students is the inclusion of examples of tasks to be accomplished.

Organizational information can help students use the center efficiently. This information includes the number of students who can work at or with the center, where they are to place completed activities, what type of evaluation they must make of their work, and where they can obtain assistance. A clear statement of objectives should be included with center directions.

How Are Learning Centers Used?

Learning centers can be used in several ways. Many teachers prefer to use them initially as a supplement to the curriculum, and later to use them as an integral part of the curriculum. If centers are used as a supplement to the curriculum, they are made available for students to use after the completion of teacher-directed activities and related workbook assignments, dittoed pages, or chalkboard tasks. If centers are used as an integral part of the curriculum, they can be substituted for all or part of workbook, chalkboard, or dittoed assignments, and for certain teacher-directed activities. Some teachers prefer to use centers as a basis for organizing the curriculum. Conferences, large group and small group teacher-directed activities are then scheduled as needed.

Self-Selection/Center Assignment

Most teachers prefer to combine student self-selection of centers and center activities with teacher assignment of centers. Teacher guided self-selection is particularly recommended when certain centers have been developed to meet the needs of specific students, when centers are appropriate for some--but not all--students, when students have had little or no experience with self-selection, or when the sequence of activities within a center is of particular importance. A class assignment chart, individual assignment cards, or teacher and student conferences (group or individual) are among the techniques used to assign students to centers.

Record Keeping

Record keeping is an important evaluative and diagnostic procedure. Students should keep records of the centers or center activities they have used, the dates on which they have used them, and their progress with the activities. Individual record sheets are recommended if students are recording evaluative comments or number of items correct. Group record sheets may be used efficiently for recording the names of students who have used a specific center, and when the center was used.

Evaluation

Teachers who are using centers may wish to focus on several aspects of evaluation:
1) How effectively students work with center activities
2) How effectively students meet curriculum objectives around which centers are designed
3) Students' attitudes about the centers
4) To what extent centers include important characteristics such as clear directions, multi-level activities, and a feedback system.

For students who are using centers for the first time it is important to provide instruction which is specifically designed to assist them with tasks such as selecting appropriate centers and center activities. The teacher should assist the students to evaluate their own work, to keep records, to work with peers, and to manage their time wisely.

What Are the Advantages of Learning Centers?

Learning centers are an effective educational tool because they foster student self-direction and independence in learning. They can be designed to meet the instructional needs of individual students as well as large and small groups of students and they can be designed to appeal to student interests. They promote active involvement of students in their learning. Centers can be used by students at many different age and achievement levels. Learning centers can be designed to be consistent with existing curriculum objectives, materials, time schedules, and teaching styles.

Chapter 1

Meeting Individual Needs of Students Through Learning Centers

Learning centers can help you meet the instructional needs of every student in your classroom. Centers can assist you to provide an exciting learning environment, and can help stimulate student enthusiasm and involvement in learning. When they are combined with teacher-directed instruction and a variety of effective teaching techniques and materials, learning centers can help you, the teacher, develop an outstanding instructional program for your students.

HERE'S HOW!

You Can Use Centers
To Focus on The Development Of Basic Skills

Because centers are frequently used as "interest centers" to develop and expand students' interest, and because centers are often used on a total self-selection, free-choice basis, many teachers question their effectiveness as a means to present or reinforce basic skills. However, one of the most important and effective uses of centers is to develop and reinforce basic skills. Centers can -- and should -- be developed around the same objectives that guide planning of teacher-directed instruction and the selection of curriculum materials. Centers can be designed specifically for and assigned to students on the basis of their basic skill needs. Thus, centers should become an integral part of the instructional program in the basic skills area.

You Can Use Centers To Expand The Curriculum Without Neglecting The Regular Program

From time to time, teachers must add new curriculum areas such as health education, career awareness, and traffic safety to their regular instructional programs. In addition, current topics or special themes (e.g., holiday observances, famous Americans, community events) should be presented to students throughout the school year. It is difficult to organize instruction in such a way that new curriculum areas and special topics can be added without taking extensive time away from regular instruction.

Because learning centers are student-directed activities which can both develop and reinforce learning, they can make it possible to present current topics and cover additional curriculum areas in an effective manner without neglecting important, ongoing components of the curriculum.

These steps can help you present additional curriculum content through centers:

1. Identify objectives for content to be covered.
2. Determine which objectives to present through teacher-directed activities and which through centers.
3. Plan and construct centers.
4. Describe the new unit or topic to students in a teacher-directed setting. At this time, outline the purposes of the unit of study, and discuss the activities which will be included. Introduce the centers which have been developed and describe the ways in which students are to use them.
5. Have students use centers during their independent work time. Use of centers can be concentrated in a few days or extended over several weeks, depending on the nature of the content and the needs of the students.
6. Schedule discussion and evaluation sessions as needed. These sessions can be conducted on an individual, small, or large group basis.

You Can Use Centers To Meet Individual Student Needs For Reinforcement Of Skills and Concepts

Every teacher attempts to help students become successful learners. One key to success in learning is to provide students with enough reinforcement experiences so that they master important skills and concepts.

Learning centers can make it possible for you to provide the appropriate amount and the type of reinforcement needed by each student in your classroom, to provide this reinforcement at those times when it is most needed, and to provide it in an interesting, stimulating manner.

You Can Use Centers In Classrooms
Where There Is An Extensive Range Of Student Needs

Students within one instructional setting may represent an extensive range of abilities, skill needs, interests, learning styles, rates of learning, and work/study habits. Combining the use of learning centers with appropriate teacher-directed, small group activities can provide the means to meet the wide variety of needs which students exhibit. Centers can help individualize both the content and pacing of the curriculum for students. Rather than programming all students through the same curriculum with the major adjustment for individual needs of students being pace or rate of learning, centers can broaden and extend the curriculum for able learners. Furthermore, they can provide additional reinforcement and "relearning" experiences for less able students or students who encounter problems with specific learning tasks.

You Can Use Centers
To Facilitate Diagnostic-Prescriptive Learning

Both classroom teachers and resource teachers frequently organize their instructional programs on a diagnostic/prescriptive basis. In other words, instruction is provided on the basis of needs identified through the on-going use of diagnostic measures. Learning centers can facilitate this type of instructional program when teachers follow some or all of the steps outlined below.

1. Develop centers around diagnosed needs of students.

2. Write the center objective on all centers and center activities.

3. Include multi-level activities in centers.

4. Develop a system for assigning centers and/or specific center activities to students.

5. Develop a record keeping system for centers.

6. Devise a procedure for students to use in recording their progress and/or reactions.

7. Observe students as they work at centers. Note their learning strengths and needs.

8. Schedule student/teacher discussion sessions to evaluate both students' work habits with centers and the quality of the tasks which they perform in centers.

9. Use information about students' work habits with centers and the quality of their performance with center tasks when preparing written evaluations of each student's perform-

ance (e.g., report cards, narrative progress reports, skill checklists).

You Can Use Centers To Help Students Set Realistic Goals And Make Decisions About Their Learning

Learning centers offer many opportunities for students to make decisions. Teachers can help students with the process of goal setting and decision making at the same time they are helping them develop skills and concepts through centers. Here are some of the decisions students can make when they use centers.

1. Which centers shall I select?
2. How many centers can I get finished in the time I have?
3. Which center shall I do first?
4. Which center activities shall I do?
5. When a center activity gives me a choice of things to do, which shall I select?
6. What materials should I bring to the center?
7. Should I work with someone?
8. What should I do if I don't want to finish an activity?
9. What should I do if I have a problem?
10. When should I ask for help?
11. Whom should I ask for help?
12. Is this center too easy...too hard?
13. What shall I do if I don't get finished?
14. What should I do with my completed work?
15. How well did I work at this center?

A strategy to follow in helping students develop decision making skills might include these steps:

- Work with students to identify specific types of decisions which they must make about using centers.
- Work with students to list possible alternatives for the decisions they must make.
- Help students estimate the amount of time needed for various types of activities.
- Help students develop a procedure to follow if they have problems with a center activity.
- Help students develop a schedule for using centers.
- Help students identify a step-by-step procedure to follow in using centers: e.g.,

  1. Select a center or find the center which has been assigned to you.
  2. Read the directions.

3. Get any materials you need.
4. Complete the tasks.
5. Check your work.
6. Put the center away carefully.
7. Record your progress, and plan what you need to do next.

It is very important to develop and discuss these strategies with students, to practice them frequently, and to evaluate progress continually.

You Can Use Centers To Assist Absentee Students And New Students

Learning centers can help you "fill in the gaps" for students who have been absent from school and for students who come to your classroom from other schools or school systems.

Centers can provide continuity in instruction for students who have been absent from school for various lengths of time. Center helpers (students who help peers with center activities) can assist returning students to select and use appropriate centers, and can help them solve problems which they may encounter. In some cases, compact centers might be sent home to be used by a student who is recovering from an illness.

Because every school does not follow the same curriculum, and does not organize instruction around the same scope and sequence of skills, some students who transfer from other schools to your classroom may need supplemental instruction before they can work comfortably with their new classmates. Learning centers can help you prepare these students for the curriculum experiences underway in your classroom.

You Can Use Centers To Motivate Students Who May Be "Turned Off" To Learning Experiences

Because learning centers can be designed to focus upon the interests of students, centers provide highly motivating learning experiences for students. Many students who have been uninterested or "turned off" by traditional instructional materials become enthusiastic about using learning centers in which they can work on activities related to their interests. For students who have experienced failure with conventional instructional materials, learning centers provide an opportunity for a fresh start with new and appropriate materials. The suggestions which follow offer ideas to help you develop highly motivating centers.

1. Determine the interests of students in your class through using a questionnaire, discussion groups, or having students construct an "interest collage" or scrapbook.
2. Have students prepare illustrations or cut pictures which interest them from magazines and newspapers. These illustrations and pictures can be placed on center materials such as folders, boxes, envelopes, bulletin boards, or partitions to make them more appealing and interesting to students.
3. Incorporate high interest materials, such as cartoons, articles, and stories from childrens magazines, word and number puzzles, functional reading materials (e.g. telephone books, TV guides, labels, menus), and commercial games (e.g., Yatze, Scrabble, Sorry) in center activities whenever possible. (See Chapter 4)
4. Incorporate manipulative devices in center activities whenever possible. (Chapter 5)
5. Use audio-visual equipment, such as language masters, tape recorders, and overhead projectors in centers to provide variety and stimulate student interest in center activities.
6. Encourage students to make centers for their peers or for younger students.

You Can Use Centers To Meet The Needs Of The Intermediate Student With Reading Problems

Intermediate students with poor reading skills need a "second chance for success" in learning basic skills, and need opportunities to keep pace with their peers in content area classes. Many of these students need to develop independent work/study skills, and a positive attitude toward themselves as learners. Regardless of the causes of their reading problems, these students share a need for success with learning experiences. Learning centers are an especially effective teaching tool to use with intermediate students with poor reading skills.

Chapter 4 describes how to use learning centers to meet the

instructional needs of intermediate students with poor reading skills.

You Can Use Centers
To Meet The Needs Of Exceptional Students

Learning centers offer an excellent means to provide instruction for exceptional students who are found in every school. The gifted student, the student with specific language disabilities, and the slow learner, all can use learning centers successfully.

Chapter 3 describes how to use learning centers to meet the instructional needs of exceptional children.

Summary

You can put centers to work in your classroom! You can use them to present basic skills and to extend the curriculum. Centers can help you provide appropriate reinforcement activities which enable students to master skills and concepts. Centers can help you to plan for a wide range of student needs, and to focus on the specific needs of students in your classroom. Centers can be used to help direct students to make decisions and set realistic goals.

Chapter 2

Learning Center Ideas

Introduction

To help you develop centers which are appropriate for your students, this chapter presents more than forty detailed descriptions of complete learning centers. Center ideas covering the curriculum areas of reading, language arts, mathematics, science, and social studies are included. Many of the centers are interdisciplinary in scope. Some of the centers can be used on a year-round, on-going basis. Included within the chapter are centers which are appropriate for each grade level, K-8.

The centers described in the chapter are multi-level, and include a variety of manipulative devices. Each center description includes the directions which students are to follow in completing the center activities. All the centers have been designed to be appealing and motivating to students.

Each center description includes the following information:

Title
Titles have been selected on the basis of their appeal to students and their appropriateness to the center objectives.

Area of Curriculum
The area of the curriculum for which the center has been designed is indicated.

Purpose of the Center
The center description states whether the center is designed to introduce, develop, or reinforce skills and concepts and/or to stimulate and extend student interests.

Suggested Grade Level
A grade level span is suggested for each center. However, ideas within any center might be adapted or adjusted to other grade levels.

Objectives
The objectives listed in each center description state specifically what the student will accomplish at the center.

Materials

Each center idea includes a complete description of the materials to be used in that center. All materials are easily accessible or very simple to construct. Materials are listed according to the activity in which they are to be used.

Introductory Material for Students

Some type of introduction or background information should be provided for students before they begin to use a center. Examples of this type of information is included in some of the center ideas.

Directions

Complete directions for each activity are included in the center description. The directions are short, simple, and student oriented.

Each center activity also includes its own title which indicates the task to be accomplished by that activity.

Evaluation

Each center idea includes a description of how activities within the center are to be evaluated. Most of the activities are self-correcting in order to provide immediate reinforcement of correct responses and to enable students to continue to work independently.

How To Select The Centers Which You Would Like To Use In Your Classroom

These questions may serve as guidelines to help you select those centers which are appropriate for use in your classroom:

	Yes	No
1. Will I be presenting this skill or concept to my students?		
2. Are the objectives appropriate for my students' instructional needs?		
3. Is the center appropriate for the age/grade level of my students?		
4. Will the activities appeal to the interests of my students?		
5. Will the center fit into my existing plans for presenting that skill or concept to students?		

How To Adjust Center Ideas To Meet Your Students' Needs

The center ideas presented in this chapter can be adjusted in numerous ways to make them appropriate to meet the instructional needs of your students. Here's how.

1. The number of activities within a center may be adjusted. Activities may be added or deleted, as appropriate.
2. The level of difficulty of the tasks may be increased or decreased. (E.g., students might record a response or draw a picture rather than writing a response. Or, students might listen to information rather than reading it.)
3. Directions may be simplified or made more detailed.
4. The center format and materials might be adapted to different content. (E.g., Spelling Practice Center, p. 25 activities and materials could be used to develop handwriting or mathematics skills.)
5. The theme may be changed. For example, students may prefer motorcycles and cars to animals, or football to baseball.
6. The quantity, type, or difficulty level of materials may be adjusted.
7. Commercial materials may be substituted for teacher-made materials.
8. The method of evaluation may be changed. (E.g., an activity could be teacher-corrected instead of student-corrected.)
9. The packaging format may be changed to make the center more or less compact.

How To Add Organization and Management (Housekeeping) Information To Help Students Use The Centers Efficiently

You may wish to add the following type of information to your centers to help students use them efficiently:

1. Number of students who can work at or with the center.
2. Where and how students can obtain help.
3. Where completed activities are to be placed.
4. How and where center materials are to be returned after students have completed center activities.
5. How completed tasks should be recorded.

Area: Language Arts

Purpose: To reinforce the language usage skill of identifying antecedents

Suggested Grade Levels: 2-4

Objective: Students will identify the correct antecedent for pronouns used in sentences and paragraphs.

Material: paper and pencil

For Activity A:

- Pocket cards presenting sentences which include both a noun and an underlined pronoun referring to that noun.
- Tab cards presenting the antecedent for the underlined pronoun used in each sentence.

For Activity B:

- Acetate covered cards presenting short, descriptive paragraphs containing several nouns and pronouns referring to those nouns. Each card should contain a statement such as "Underline all the pronouns which refer to Tom."

For Activity C:

- A story of high-interest containing several nouns and related pronouns. Number each pronoun in the story.

For Activity D:

- grease pencils   • acetate covers

Directions

Activity A - *Identifying Antecedents*

1. Read the sentences on the pocket card.
2. Locate the underlined pronoun.
3. Find the tab card with the word to which the pronoun refers. This is the antecedent.
4. Place the tab card in the pocket card.
5. Check your work.

Activity B - *Finding Pronouns*

1. Read each paragraph.
2. Underline all the pronouns which refer to the noun listed at the top of the card.
3. Check your work.

Activity C - *Matching Pronouns and Antecedents*

1. Read the paragraph.
2. Study the underlined words, and identify the antecedent for each.
3. Number your paper.
4. Beside each number, write the antecedent to which the pronoun with the same number refers.

Activity D - *Writing Antecedents*

1. Write a short story. Don't forget to use antecedents.
2. Place your story under an acetate cover.
3. Make a separate answer key. List the pronouns and antecedents.
4. Ask a classmate to read the story and to underline the pronouns and antecedents.
5. Discuss the answers.
6. Take your paper from the acetate cover and place it and the answer key in the folder.

Evaluation: Activity A, answers on the backs of the pocket cards.

Activities B and C, separate answer keys.

Activity D, peer discussion and teacher correction.

How To Build Good Listening Skills

Area: Language Arts

Purpose: To reinforce listening skills

Suggested Grade Levels: 3-4

Objectives: Students will identify reasons why we listen.
Students will describe how to listen effectively.
Students will listen to taped selections for specific purposes.
Students will answer questions based upon what they have heard.

Materials: paper and pencil

For Activity A:

• list of things we listen to (E.g., television programs, music, teacher's directions, telephone conversations, class discussions...)
• list of reasons why we listen (E.g., to learn, to find out where to go or what to do, for enjoyment, for safety purposes, for understanding, to get information)

For Activity B:

• cards which list something to which we listen

telephone message telling where to meet your mother	directions to someone's house where you are to go

background music	instructions on how to stop bleeding	information for a test

For Activity C:

• tape recorder
• taped directions for doing things such as making a puppet, finding a store, etc.

Directions

Activity A - *Why Do We Listen?*

1. Make a list of things you listen to.
2. Compare your list with the list in the folder. Add to the list in the folder any new ideas you may have.
3. Make a list of reasons why you listen.
4. Compare your list to the list in the folder.

Activity B - *How Should We Listen?*

1. Think about these things:
   • Do you need to listen to everything in the same way?
   • Are there some things to which you must listen more carefully than others? Why?
2. Get the envelope marked "How Should You Listen?"
3. Read the item on each card. How should you listen to each thing listed?
4. Write each of the items on a sheet of paper. Beside each item, write **how** you should listen in that situation, and why you feel that way.

Activity C - *Get Ready to Listen*

Two stories have been taped on the cassette.

1. Before each story you will hear purposes or reasons for listening to the stories. These purposes will get you ready to listen to the stories. After each story you will hear questions about the story that will help you decide how well you listened.
2. Turn on the tape and listen carefully.
4. Answer the questions at the end of the tape.

Note: These answers could be written on a sheet of paper, or recorded on tape.

Activity D - *Listen Very Carefully*

1. Work with a partner.
2. Several sets of directions have been taped on the cassette.
3. Listen very carefully to each separate set of directions. You will want to remember all of the steps in each set.
4. After you have listened to each set of directions, describe them to your partner.
5. Have your partner check your directions by looking at the answer key.

Evaluation: Activities A and C, self-check.
Activity B, teacher correction.
Activity D, peer evaluation.

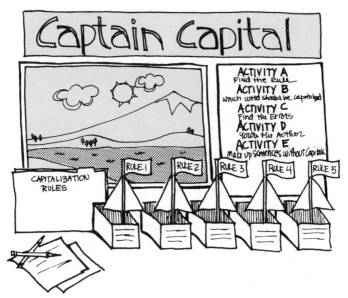

Area: Language Arts

Purpose: To reinforce the language usage skill of capitalization

To reinforce the correct usage of capitalization rules

Suggested Grade Levels: 3-5

Objectives: Students will match sentences containing capitalized words with statements of capitalization rules.

Students will identify words that should be capitalized in sentences in which no capital letters have been used.

Students will identify words within a paragraph which have been incorrectly capitalized.

Students will follow capitalization rules in writing a short paragraph describing a picture.

Materials: *For Activity A:*

•A set of cans or boxes on each of which is placed a capitalization rule.

•A set of sentence cards, each card presenting a sentence in which the words have been correctly capitalized. One capitalized word per sentence is underlined.

> Sarah lives in <u>Tennessee.</u>

For Activity B:

•A set of sentence cards, each card presenting a sentence with no capital letters.

•A folder listing capitalization rules which students have studied.

For Activity C:

•A set of paragraphs - each paragraph presenting some words which are incorrectly capitalized.

For Activity D:
•A picture of interest to students
•pencils   •paper

Directions

Activity A - *Find the Rule*
1. Read the capitalization rule on each can (box).
2. Read each sentence. Study the underlined word in the sentence.
3. Place the sentence in the can that states the rule which explains why the underlined word has been capitalized.
4. Check your work.

Activity B - *Which Words Should Be Capitalized?*
1. Read each sentence carefully.
2. Decide which words should be capitalized.
3. Look at the rules in the folder if you need help.
4. Check your work.

Activity C - *Find the Errors*
1. Read each paragraph carefully.
2. List the words which are capitalized incorrectly.
3. Look at the rules in the folder. Decide which rule explains why the word is capitalized incorrectly. List the number of the rule.
4. Check your work.

Activity D - *You're the Author*
1. Write a paragraph describing the picture.
2. Check your work to be certain you have followed capitalization rules correctly.
3. Place your paragraph in the folder.

Activity E - *Make Up Sentences Without Capitals*
1. Write ten sentences, but do not capitalize any of the words in your sentences.
2. Make an answer key showing which words should be capitalized.
3. Have a classmate write the words to be capitalized in your sentences.
4. Together, compare the words to the answer key.

Evaluation: Activity A - self-check, separate answer key or answers on backs of cans (boxes).
Activities B and C - self-check, separate answer key or answers on backs of cards.
Activities D and E - teacher correction or self-check.

Area: Language Arts

Purpose: To provide a stimulus for creative writing

Suggested Grade Levels: 4-6

Objectives: Students will write episodes for TV programs involving their favorite character.

Students will write a summary of their episode for a "TV Newsletter".

Students will describe a favorite episode from a TV program.

Materials: •paper •pencils •dictionaries

•A bulletin board, or charts covered with TV schedules, pictures of TV personalities, and names of TV shows.

Introduction: Think about your favorite television program. This center is about your favorite program!

Directions

Activity A - *Which Program is Your Favorite?*

1. What is your favorite TV program?
2. Which episode from your favorite program did you like best?
3. Write a description of your favorite episode.
4. Illustrate what you thought was the best part of the program.

Note: Group discussion of a script format would be helpful before beginning Activity B.

Activity B - *Write a Script for an Episode of Your Favorite TV program*

1. Think about how the characters in your favorite TV program act, speak, and think.
2. Make an outline of a script for an episode of your favorite TV program.

3. Write the script for the show you are planning.
4. You may wish to include notes about scenery or costumes, and comments about how the characters should speak, stand, or act.
5. Give your script to a friend to read. Ask your friend for suggestions.
6. Put your script in the folder for editing.
7. After your script is edited, make a final corrected copy.

Activity C - *Prepare a Description of Your Program for a TV Schedule*

1. Read the descriptions of TV programs which appear in TV schedules. The descriptions are short, and present a main idea.
2. Write a description of your TV program episode that could appear in a TV schedule.
3. Put your description in the folder.

Evaluation: Activity A, teacher correction.
Activity B, peer discussion and teacher correction.
Activity C, teacher correction.

Area: Language Arts

Purpose: To reinforce speaking skills

Suggested Grade Levels: 4-6

Objectives: Students will prepare and present a description of how to do something.

Students will prepare and present a talk designed to persuade others to buy or to do something.

Students will prepare and present a report which compares and contrasts information from two different sources.

Materials: •paper   •tape recorder
•pencil   •chart listing tips for effective speaking

Note: It is recommended that students contribute to the development of this chart.

Sample:

TIPS FOR EFFECTIVE SPEAKING
1. Select a topic which interests you.
2. Think about the topic.
3. List what you want to say.
4. Organize your ideas so they are in the right order.
5. Make an outline.
6. Prepare charts, pictures, or diagrams, if you wish.
7. Practice your speech.
8. Make any needed changes.
9. Speak clearly.
10. Look at your audience.

For Activity C:
•reference materials such as textbooks or encyclopedia

Activity A - *How Do You Do It?*

1. Select a topic which you could describe to your classmates. Here are some suggestions:
   - How to bake a cake
   - How to ride a ten-speed bike
   - How to train a dog
   - How to keep score in bowling
   - How to care for a guinea pig
   - How to fly a kite
2. List any steps you would follow.
3. Make any diagrams or pictures which may help your audience understand how to do what you are describing.
4. Practice your description with a friend or record it on the tape recorder.
5. Sign the "How Do You Do It?" sheet when you are ready to present your description to the class.

Activity B - *Try It - You'll Like It!*

1. Select something which you could persuade your classmates to do or to buy. Here are some suggestions:
   - Join a softball team
   - Read a specific book (your choice)
   - Buy a specific record album (your choice)
   - Join a club
   - Vote for a specific person
   - Buy a certain brand of toothpaste
   - Buy a certain type of car
2. Outline the things you will say to persuade your classmates to do or to buy what you are suggesting.
3. Make posters or banners if you feel they will help you be more persuasive.
4. Practice your speech with a friend or record it on the tape recorder.
5. Sign the "Try It - You'll Like It" sheet when you are ready to give your speech to the class.

Activity C - *Two Points of View*

1. Select a question or issue on which there are at least two different points of view. Here are some suggestions:
   - The Conservation of Energy
   - The Problem of Crime in Our Area
   - The High Cost of Running a School
   - The School Year Should Be 12 Months Long
2. Describe different points of view about the problem or issue which you have selected. Use the references to help you.
3. Prepare a speech which clearly presents these different points of view.
4. Make charts or diagrams if you feel they will make your speech more clear.
5. Practice your speech with a friend or record it on tape.
6. Sign the "Two Points of View" sheet when you are ready to present your speech to the class.

Evaluation: Activities A-C, teacher evaluation.

Area: Language Arts

Purpose: To promote creative writing

Suggested Grade Levels:

Objectives: Students will write stories on topics of their choice.

Students will bind stories they have written.

Students will develop book jackets for books they have read.

Students will develop brochures or catalogues advertising books they have read.

Note: This center could be adapted to younger grade levels by eliminating the "Advertising Department" and changing "Book Jacket Design Area" to "Art Department." Have students design picture books.

Materials: •paper •crayons, paints or magic markers •pencils •heavy tape •cardboard

For Activity A:

•"Idea Starter Kit" for author containing story titles.

For Activity B:

•Chart giving directions on how to bind a book.

Directions

Activity A - *Author's Room*

1. Select a topic for your book. If you need some suggestions, look in the "Idea Starter Kit" for suggestions.
2. Make an outline for your book. Divide your book into chapters.
3. Write your book.
4. Make a title page for your book.

5. Make illustrations to go with your book.
6. Put it in the editor's file so your teacher can schedule an editor's conference.
7. Edit your story after your editor's conference with the teacher.

Activity B - *Binding Department*

1. Select the type of cover you want for your book.
2. Design your cover.
3. Follow directions on the chart for binding books.
4. Prepare a library card and envelope for the back of your book so it can be checked in and out.

Activity C: *Book Jacket Design Area*

1. Design a book jacket for your book.
2. Design a picture for the cover.
3. Write a summary of your book on one inside flap of the book jacket.
4. Write a short paragraph about yourself, the author, on the other inside flap of the book jacket.

Activity D: *Advertising Department*

1. Identify what you consider to be the best parts of your book.
2. Design an ad that you think would make someone want to buy your book. Include what you like best about your book in the ad.
3. Illustrate your ad.

Evaluation: Discussion between student and teacher.

Note: This center can be used throughout the year with little maintenance except keeping construction supplies available.

Area: Language Arts, Art

Purpose: To reinforce skills in creative writing
To reinforce handwriting skills
To stimulate and extend interests in art (or artistic expression)

Suggested Grade Levels: 1-6

Objectives: Students will design a greeting card.
Students will write an appropriate verse or message for the greeting card.

Materials:

- Construction paper
- Water color paints
- Crayons
- Magic markers
- Glue
- List of words such as birthday, anniversary, illness, holiday, etc.
- Fronts of old greeting cards
- Bits of yarn, ribbon, lace
- Small pieces of cloth
- Pieces of foil
- Scraps of gift wrap
- Newsprint
- Chart giving directions for making an envelope by folding and pasting construction paper

Directions

Activity A - *Do It Yourself*

1. Think about the person who will receive your card. What does he or she enjoy doing?
2. Sketch the design for your greeting card on newsprint.
3. Create a verse or message for your card on the newsprint. You may write a poem or a note.
4. Ask a friend to look at your card design and offer suggestions, if you wish.
5. Select the materials you will need to make your card.
6. Create your card.

7. Write the verse or note inside the card, or on a separate sheet of paper which you place inside the card.
8. Make an envelope for your card by following the directions on the chart.

Evaluation:

Note: Encourage students to bring scraps of yarn, foil, lace, cloth, and ribbon as well as pictures from old greeting cards to keep card construction supplies fresh and changing. The greeting card center could have a "holiday" theme for special days such as Valentine's Day.

Area: Language Arts
Purpose: To reinforce skills in spelling words
Suggested Grade Levels: 1-8
Objectives: Students will practice words through using a variety of techniques.

Note: Only those materials which are needed for the activities you select for the center will be needed.

Materials:
- language master
- tape recorder
- acetate envelopes
- magic slates
- magic markers
- newsprint
- oak tag
- glue
- yarn
- aerosol can of shaving cream and metal cookie tray
- individual chalkboards
- magazines and newspapers
- dictionary
- list of "story starter" titles

Introduction: There are many ways in which you can study and practice your spelling words. The important thing is that you do practice them. This center can help!

Directions

1. Read the "Idea Cards" that explain ways in which you can study your words.
2. Decide how you would like to study your words.
3. Get the materials you need.
4. Study your words.
5. Put the materials away when you are finished.

Example of "Idea Cards"

Make a Crossword Puzzle from your Spelling Words
1. Write your words in the form of a crossword puzzle.
2. Number the crossword puzzle.
3. Write definitions for the words.
4. Exchange definitions with a classmate.
5. Complete the classmate's puzzle.

Write Your Words on the Acetate Envelope
1. Copy your spelling words on cards.
2. Put one card in the acetate envelope at a time.
3. Trace the word on the envelope with the grease pencil until you think you remember it.
4. Turn the acetate envelope on the back and write the word from memory.
5. Check your word. If it is correct, choose another word to practice.

Make Your Spelling Words 3-D!
1. Write your word on a card.
2. Trace over the word with glue.
3. Make your word "3-D" by putting yarn, bird seed, beans or string on the glue.
4. Practice with a friend.

Write Your Words in Shaving Cream
1. Carefully spread a thin layer of shaving cream over the pan.
2. Write your spelling words in the shaving cream with your finger.
3. Use paper towels to clean the tray when you are finished.

Use the Tape Recorder or Language Master to Record Your Spelling Words
1. Say your word.
2. Spell your word.
3. Say the word again.
4. Check yourself.

Use the Dictionary!
Use the dictionary to help you divide your spelling words into syllables and write their meanings.

Make a Word Quiz
The man walked *briskly*.

a. slowly
b. rapidly
c. carefully

Write a Story!
Use your spelling words in a story, poem, play or article. The "Story Starters" in the envelope will get you started if you need some ideas.

Write Your Words...
- on the chalkboard
- on the magic slate
- on the newsprint with magic markers

Make a Spelling Collage
Find your spelling words in newspapers and magazines. Make a collage with them.

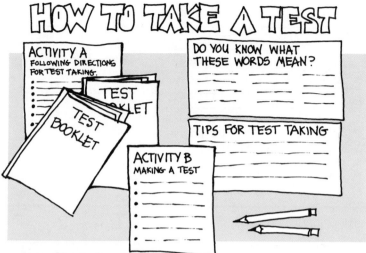

Area: Interdisciplinary

Purpose: To reinforce skills involved in test taking

Suggested Grade Levels: 3-8

Objectives: Students will practice skills involved in taking tests.

Students will work with various types of formats for test items (multiple choice, completion, matching, true-false, essay).

Materials: *For Activity A*

•Dittoed test booklets made from worksheets containing various types of test items.

••All test items on a worksheet should be presented in the same format; e.g., multiple choice, completion, matching, true-false, essay.

••Use very simple, well understood content since the purpose is to help students use various types of test item formats.

••Include directions and an example on each worksheet.

••Grade level and skill needs of students should determine the specific content of the test items, and the number of items per worksheet.

••Cover the worksheets with acetate if individual booklets are not available.

•Answer keys

•Reference chart of hints for test taking

> **TIPS FOR TEST TAKING**
> •Listen to or read the directions very carefully.
> •Study examples which are given.
> •Do easy questions first.
> •Review your answers if you have time.

•Separate answer sheets for multiple choice test items
(Answer Sheet)

Name _____

Last   First

Date _____
School _____
Grade_____Teacher _____

1. A B C D   7. A B C D
2. A B C D   8. A B C D
3. A B C D   9. A B C D
4. A B C D   10. A B C D
5. A B C D   11. A B C D
6. A B C D   12. A B C D

•Reference chart of words frequently used on tests

DO YOU KNOW WHAT THESE WORDS MEAN?

match	order	write
select	best answer	fill in the blanks
circle	opposite	shade
mark	underline	check

•Examples of directions and item formats which can be used for worksheets

1. Match words in Column A with their opposites in Column B by putting a number from column B on the blank line before each word in column A.
   Sample:

A	B
_3_ fat	1. out
_5_ happy	2. cold
_4_ up	3. thin
_1_ in	4. down
	5. sad
	6. stop

2. Select the number in Column A which belongs in each set in Column B.
   Sample:

A	B
a. 3, 5, 7, 8	2, 4, 6, **8,** 10
b. 1, 5, 6, 10	3, **6,** 9, 12, 15
c. 13, 14, 15, 16	5, 10, **15,** 20, 25

3. For each sentence below underline T if the sentence is true, and F if the sentence is false.

   T _F_ Plants need no water to grow.

4. Circle the word which begins like the picture beside each line of words.
   Sample:

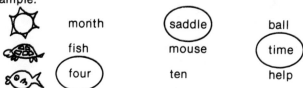

	month	saddle	ball
	fish	mouse	time
	four	ten	help

5. Make an X in the box next to the word that means the same thing as (is the synonym of) the underlined word in the phrase at the left.
   Sample.
   The **tiny** mouse ran away.
   - [ ] small
   - [ ] large
   - [ ] bring
   - [ ] child

6. Write in the box the number which is beside the word that makes the sentence correct.
   Sample:
   A nickel is equal to 10¢. ☐
   1. never
   2. sometimes
   3. always

7. Fill in the blanks with the words that fit best.
   Sample:
   Hat is to **head** as shoe is to foot.

8. Number each set of sentences to show the order in which things happen.
   _2_ Put film in the camera.
   _4_ Develop the film.
   _1_ Buy the film.
   _3_ Take pictures
   _5_ Show the pictures to friends.

9. Read each paragraph. Read the questions which follow the paragraph. Select the best answer for each question. Darken the letter beside the best answer on your answer sheet.

Jupiter is the biggest planet. It is more than ten times bigger than the Earth. It has an atmosphere of poisonous gases. It does not have oxygen or water. It is very, very cold. Jupiter has twelve moons.

   1. Which word in the story means "air"?
      a. planet
      b. atmosphere
      c. poisonous

2. How many moons does Jupiter have?
   a. 10
   b. none
   c. 12
3. How does Jupiter compare with the Earth in size?
   a. It is about the same.
   b. It is ten times bigger.
   c. It is twelve times smaller.

Introduction:

This center will help you follow directions when you take tests or complete written assignments. It has many different kinds of directions and questions, so work carefully!

Directions

Activity A - *Following Directions for Test Items*

1. Get a test booklet.
2. Read the directions on each page very carefully.
3. Study the example on each page.
4. Do the items on each page. They will not be hard for you.
5. Look back over the page to check your work.
6. Check your work with the answer key.
7. Go on to the next page in your booklet.

Activity B - *Making A Test*

1. Plan a test on something which you have studied recently.
2. Decide what to ask questions about.
3. Decide what format you want to use for your test items. Will you use multiple choice, true-false, matching, completion, essay, or a combination?
4. Write your test.
5. Make your answer key.
6. Put your test and answer key in the folder.

Evaluation: Activity A - self-checking, separate answer keys. Activity B - teacher correction.

LEARN·A·LETTER

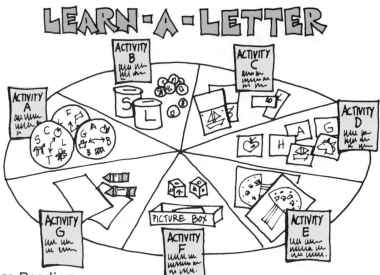

Area: Reading

Purpose: To reinforce letter-sound (phonics) associations

Suggested Grade Levels: K-1

Objectives: Students will match letters with pictures which begin with those letters.

Students will match letters with pictures which end with those letters.

Materials: CONSTRUCTION SUGGESTIONS FOR THESE MATERIALS CAN BE FOUND IN CHAPTER 5.

For Activity A - *Letter/Sound Clocks*
(letters and pictures on a clock face)

For Activity B - *Letter/Sound Banks with Picture Coins*
(coffee cans with plastic lids having slots cut in the lids)

For Activity C - *Letter/Sound Pockets*

For Activity D - *Letter/Sound Concentration Cards*

For Activity E - *Letter/Sound Mushrooms*

For Activity F - *Letter Cube*

Note: The number of different letters included in each activity should be determined by the number of letters to which the students have been introduced.

Directions

Activity A - *Match the Pictures to the Letters*

1. Get a clock.
2. Look at the pictures on the clock.
3. Read the letters on the clock.
4. Move the hands of the clock to match each picture with its beginning letters.
5. Check your work.

Activity B - *Match the Pictures to the Letters*
1. Read the letters on the banks.
2. Look at the pictures on the coins in the coin box.
3. Put the coin pictures in the bank with their beginning letter.
4. Check your work.
5. Put the coins back in the coin box.

Activity C - *Match the Pictures to the Letters*
1. Read the question on each card.
2. Look at the pictures.
3. Read the letters on the tab cards.
4. Match the pictures with their beginning letters.
5. Check your work.

Activity D - *Match the Pictures to the Letters*
1. Get a set of concentration cards.
2. Work with a partner.
3. Play concentration by matching letters and pictures.
4. Check your work.

Activity E - *Match the Pictures to the Letters*
1. Get a mushroom.
2. Work with a partner.
3. Punch a picture.
4. Say the picture name and its beginning letter.
5. Ask your partner if you are right.

Activity F - *Match the Pictures to the Letters*
1. Roll the cube.
2. Read the letter on top.
3. Find as many words from the picture box as you can that begin with that letter.
4. Check your work.

Activity G - *Make Your Own Clock*
1. Make your own letter clock using these letters: m, s, b, f.

Evaluation: Activity A - Self-correction, answers on the backs of the clocks.

Activity B - Self-correction, answers on backs of banks or separate answer key.

Activity C - Self-correction, answers on backs of pocket cards.

Activities D and F - Self-correction, answers on separate answer key.

Activity E - Self-correction, answers on back of mushroom.

Activity G - Teacher correction.

Note: The center ideas can be used with ending consonants, vowels, or blends.

Area: Reading

Purpose: To reinforce skills involved in classifying and categorizing

Suggested Grade Levels: K-2

Objectives: Students will match items with categories.
Students will place items into categories.

Materials:

For Activity A:
- pictures of items which fit specific categories: e.g., cars, toys, foods, flowers, animals, clothing.
- category titles to go with the items above

For Activity B:
- "Which One Doesn't Fit?" category picture cards. Each card includes four items which fit a particular category and one which does not.

For Activity C:
- category titles which students will use to find items that fit the categories (e.g., things with wheels, red things, things that break, soft things, rough things, things that taste sweet.)

For Activity D:
- box of small items which can fit into specific categories (e.g., small toys, school supplies, hardware, household items)
- paper • pencils • crayons • magazines

Introduction: How are things alike? How are they different?
We ask these questions when we classify things.
This center will give you practice putting things into categories.

Directions

Activity A - *Match Pictures with Words*

1. Look at the pictures.
2. Look at the words.
3. Match the pictures with the words.
4. Check your work by looking on the back of the pictures.

Activity B - *Which Picture Doesn't Fit?*

1. Take the picture cards from Box B.
2. Look at the five pictures on each card.
3. One picture does not belong with the others.
4. Which picture is different?
5. Check your work by looking on the back.

Activity C - *Finish Each Category*

1. Take the category titles from Envelope C.
2. Read the category titles.
3. Find or draw pictures of at least five things to fit each title.

Activity D - *Name the Category*

1. Arrange the items into groups according to something that is alike about each item in the group.
2. Make a title for each group.
3. Make a chart showing the titles of the groups and all the items in the group.

Evaluation: Activities A and B - Self-correction on back.
Activities C and D - Teacher correction.

BEFORE OR AFTER?

Area: Reading

Purpose: To reinforce students' ability to identify sequence of events

Suggested Grade Levels: 2-4

Objectives: Students will determine whether events in a story happened before or after a certain key event.

Materials: *For Activity A*

- A set of manila envelopes, each containing a comic strip which has been cut into separate frames. On the front of each envelope is one of the frames from the strip inside that envelope. (Vary which frame is selected.)

For Activity B

- A high-interest story at students' reading level which includes a sequence of events placed in a folder.
- A set of cards, each card listing one event in the story.
- Two boxes...one labeled "BEFORE" and one labeled "AFTER".

For Activity C

- pictures in a folder showing some type of action.

Directions

Activity A - *What Happens Next?*

1. Select an envelope and look at the comic strip frame on the front of the envelope. This is the key picture.
2. Take the rest of the frames from the envelope.
3. Place the frames which you think show what happened before the key picture to the left of the key picture.
4. Place the frames which you think happened after the key picture to the right of the picture.
5. Check your work. Complete the activities in the remaining envelopes in the same way.

Activity B - *Before or After?*

1. Read the story in the folder.
2. Read the key event written on the front of the folder.
3. Read the events on the cards.
4. If the event on the card takes place before the key event, place it in the "BEFORE" box.
5. If the event on the card takes place after the key event, place it in the "AFTER" box.
6. Check your work.

Activity C - *Drawing Before and After*

1. Look at the pictures in the folder.
2. Decide what has happened before the activity you see in the picture, and what you think will happen next.
3. Draw two pictures...one showing what might have happened before, and one showing what may happen next.
4. Put your pictures in the "Finished Work" folder.

Evaluation: Activities A and B: Self-check, answers on the backs of the pictures and cards.
Activity C: Teacher correction.

Note: The difficulty of this center can be controlled through the type of comics (number of frames, level of sophistication of the comic strip, amount of inference required to determine the "plot") and difficulty of the stories which are selected.
Motivational appeal can be heightened through the type of material selected. (What are students' favorite comics?)

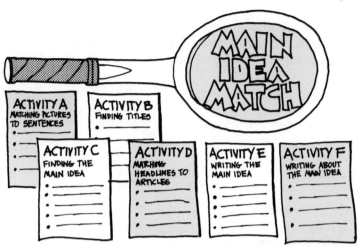

Note: Paragraphs and pictures could be related to a specific theme of interest to students. Paragraphs could be based upon content in social studies, science, literature, etc.

Area: Reading

Purpose: To reinforce comprehension skills in the area of main idea.

Suggested Grade Levels: 3-5

Objectives: Given a picture or reading selection, students will identify the main idea of the selection.

Materials: paper and pencil

For Activity A:
• pictures showing some type of action
• descriptive sentences which correspond to the pictures

For Activity B:
• short paragraphs of interest to students
• title cards which correspond to the paragraphs

For Activity C:
• pocket cards containing short paragraphs with three related statements, one of which is the main idea of the paragraph.
• cards written A, B, or C

For Activity D:
• newspaper articles of interest to students (articles from children's newspapers could be used)
• headlines from these articles mounted on separate cards

For Activity E:
• short stories for which students are to provide titles and illustrations

Note: Pictures and paragraphs can be cut from old workbooks or dittoes; they can be teacher developed, or students can make them.
• cubes containing main idea statements related to specific areas of interest

Introduction: A main idea tells you what a picture, a paragraph, or a story is about. This center will help you identify the main idea of things you read.

Directions

Activity A - *Matching Pictures to Sentences*

1. Look at the pictures.
2. Read the sentences.
3. Match each picture with the sentences which describe it.
4. Check your work by looking on the back of the cards.

Activity B - *Finding Titles*

1. Read the titles.
2. Read the short paragraphs.
3. Match each paragraph with the title which states its main idea.
4. Check your work.

Activity C - *Finding the Main Idea*

1. Read the paragraphs on each pocket card.
2. Read the three statements below each paragraph.
3. Select the statement which is the main idea of the paragraph.
4. Put the appropriate letter card in the pocket.
5. Check your work.

Activity D - *Matching Headlines and Articles*

1. Read the newspaper headlines.
2. Read the newspaper articles.
3. Match the articles and headlines.
4. Check your work.

Activity E - *Writing the Main Idea*

1. Get the story folder, a sheet of paper, and a pencil. Number your paper.
2. Read the stories.
3. Decide what you think is the main idea of each story.
4. Write the main idea of each story on your paper beside the number of that story.
5. Put your paper in the folder.

Activity D - *Writing About the Main Idea*

1. Select a "main idea" cube in your interest area.
2. Roll the cube.
3. Write a story or article about the main idea on the top of the cube.
4. Put it in the folder.

Evaluation: Activities A, B and D - Self-check, answers written on the backs of the cards or headlines.

Activity C - Self-check, answers written on the backs of the pocket cards.

Activities E and F - Teacher correction

Area: Reading

Purpose: To expand vocabulary through a review of multiple meanings of words

Suggested Grade Levels: 3-5

Objectives: Students will match words having multiple meanings with their definitions.

Students will identify the correct definition for words with multiple meanings when they are used in a sentence context.

Materials: •paper •pencil •paper clips

For Activity A:

•Cards containing a set of definitions for a word with multiple meanings.
   •false teeth
   •dish
   •flat, thin piece of metal
•Cards containing words with multiple meanings (One word per card)

run		plate		rock

For Activity B

•A set of pocket cards for each word used. The definition of the word should be written at the top of the pocket card. Include as many pocket cards as definitions to be reviewed.

Set I - "Rock"

move back and forth	loud, rhythmic music	A large stone

•A set of sentence cards for each word used. Each word used in several different ways,

He threw the <u>rock</u> in the water.	<u>Rock</u> the baby to sleep.	The <u>rock</u> band was good.

Directions

Activity A - *Matching a Word to Several Meanings*
1. Read the set of definitions on each pocket card.
2. Read the words.
3. Match the word with its set of multiple meanings or definitions.
4. Check your work.

Activity B - *What Does the Word Mean in the Sentence?*
1. Read the sentences on the cards.
2. Decide which definition best describes the meaning of the under-lined word as it is used in the sentence.
3. Put the sentence card in the pocket with the correct definition.
4. Check your work.

Activity C - *Drawing the Meanings of a Word*
1. Think of a word which has at least three different meanings.
2. Draw a different picture on a separate sheet of paper for each meaning of the word. Here is an example.

3. Write the word on the back of each picture.
4. Clip all the pictures together that show the same word.
5. Put your pictures in the folder.
Note: These pictures could be drawn on a transparency by the student and used for class discussion.

Activity D - *Discover the Word*
1. Take a set of pictures from the folder.
2. Think of the word the pictures describe.
3. Turn the pictures over to check.
4. Return the pictures to the folder when finished.

Evaluation: Activity A - Self-check, answers on backs of pocket cards.

Activity B - Self-check, answers on backs of sentence cards.

Activity C - Teacher correction.

Activity D - Self-check, answers on backs of pictures.

Area: Reading

Purpose: To reinforce the study skills of using an index

Suggested Grade Levels: 3-6

Objectives: Students will use the index of a catalogue to determine if an item is listed in the index. Students will use the index of a catalogue to answer questions related to alphabetical listing of items in the index.

Students will use the index of a catalogue to find the page numbers on which specific items are located.

Materials: paper and pencil

For Activities A-C:

•Sales catalogue which contains an index
•Question cards

Sample questions for Activity A
1. Are "motorcycles" listed in the catalogue index?
2. Are "rings" listed in the index?
3. How many different kinds of "balls" are listed in the index?
4. What are they?

Sample questions for Activity B
1. Which are listed first in the catalogue, hunting supplies or toys?
2. Which are listed first in the catalogue, fabrics or furniture?
3. Would you find "boots" before or after "bikes"?

Sample questions for Activity C
1. On what pages would you find shirts?
2. On what pages would you find house paint?
3. On what pages would you find refrigerators?

Introduction:

An index can help you save time and find just what you want. Can you use the index of the catalogue to answer the questions in Activities A, B, and C?

Directions

Activities A-C - *What's in the Catalogue?*
1. Read the questions.
2. Use the index to find the answers.
3. Write the answers on a sheet of paper.
4. Check your work.

Activity D - *Where Are They Found?*
1. Select five things you would like to order from the catalogue.
2. List them in alphabetical order, as you would find them in the catalogue index.
3. Beside each item, write the page number on which it is found in the catalogue.
4. Put your paper in the folder.

Activity E - *Make Your Own Catalogue*
1. Design a mini-catalogue which includes things you like.
2. Make an index for the catalogue.
3. Show the catalogue to your teacher.

Evaluation: Activities A-C, separate answer keys. Activities D and E, teacher correction.

Area: Reading

Purpose: To reinforce the study skill of using an encyclopedia
To reinforce the comprehension skill of determining the main idea.

Suggested Grade Levels: 3-8

Objectives: Students will select from a list of questions the key words which they could use to locate answers to those questions in an encyclopedia.

Students will use the key words to determine in which volume of an encyclopedia they might look to find an answer.

Materials: paper and pencil

For Activity A:

• A set of question cards with questions such as the following:
Where was Abraham Lincoln born?
What is the largest city in Pennsylvania?
What is a Great Dane?
For what is Madam Curie famous?
What do tigers eat?
What do lasers do?

For Activity B:

• A set of encyclopedia or a sketch of a set of encyclopedia.

Directions

Activity A - *Find the Key Word*

1. Read the question on each card.
2. Select the key word or words from each question that you would use to find the answer to the question in the encyclopedia.
3. List the key word or words on your paper.
4. Check your work.

Activity B - *Locate Information*

1. Use your list from Activity A.
2. Write the number of the encyclopedia volume in which you find the answer beside each key word.
3. Check your work.

Activity C - *Try Some Research*

1. Select three questions from the question cards for which you would like to find answers.
2. Locate the answers in the encyclopedia.
3. Make notes on your paper to help you remember the answers.

Activity D - *Use Key Words to Find Answers*

1. Make a list of questions containing key words.
2. Have a friend locate the key words and find the answer to two of the questions.
3. Check and discuss the answers together.

Evaluation: Activity A: Self-check, key words listed on the back of each question card.

Activity B: Self-check, answer key listing question and appropriate encyclopedia volume.

Activity C: Teacher correction.

Activity D: Discussion.

Area: Reading

Purpose: To extend vocabulary and comprehension skills through the study of analogies

Suggested Grade Levels: 4-8

Objectives: Students will complete analogies by matching cards.

Students will describe how word pairs in analogies are related.

Students will write analogies.

Materials: •paper   •pencil

For Activity A:

•Cards containing incomplete analogies and a clue as to how the words in the analogy are related.

night : day :: Stop : _____ Clue: word opposites	Whitney : Cotton Gin :: Wright Brothers :_____ Clue: inventor, inventions	Annapolis : Md. :: Harrisburg :_____ Clue: capitals and states

For Activity B:

•Cards containing incomplete analogies only.

Shoe : Foot :: hat :	three : nine :: four :

Introduction:

Analogies tell us how things are similar. To complete an analogy, look for clues that tell how the words are related. For example, the pairs of words below are related because each pair of words are opposites.

old : young : : short : tall

Directions

Activity A - *Use the Clues to Complete the Analogies*

1. Get the set of analogy cards from Box A, a pencil and paper.
2. Read the analogy on each card. Read the clue telling how the words in the analogy are related.
3. Write the analogy on your paper.
4. Check your work.

Activity B - *How Are The Words Related?*

1. Get the set of analogy cards from Box B, a pencil and paper.
2. Read the analogy on each card.
3. Think about how the words are related.
4. Complete the analogy.
5. Check your work.

Activity C - *Write Some Analogies*

1. Think of five analogies.
2. Write your analogies on a sheet of paper.
3. Ask a friend to discuss them with you.
4. Put them in a folder.

Evaluation: Activities A and B - Self-correction, separate answer key or answers written on backs of cards.
Activity C - Teacher correction.

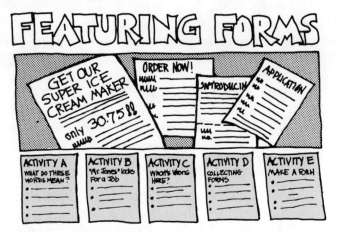

Area: Reading - Career Education

Purpose: To reinforce the functional reading vocabulary used on application and order forms

Suggested Grade Levels: 5-8

Objectives: Students will match vocabulary terms found on application forms with definitions of those terms.

Students will complete application forms using information about a fictitious person.

Students will identify errors on completed application forms.

Materials: paper and pencil

For Activity A:

•vocabulary cards with words such as business address, zip code, employer

•definition cards which correspond to the vocabulary cards

For Activity B:

•application or order forms requesting information such as name, address, phone number

•information about a "fictitious" person to be used in completing application or order forms

For Activity C:

•application or order forms which have been completed incorrectly

Note: Whenever possible, use order forms which appeal to students' interest; e.g., sports equipment, record clubs.

Directions

Activity A - *What Do These Words Mean?*

1. Read the vocabulary cards.
2. Read the definition cards.
3. Match the words with the definitions.
4. Check your work.

Activity B - *"Mr. Jones" Looks For A Job*
1. Read the information about "John Jones" in the folder.
2. Complete the application form using the information about Mr. Jones.
3. Check your work.

Activity C - *What's Wrong Here?*
1. Read the completed application form and order form in the acetate folders.
2. Find the errors and circle them with the grease pencil.
3. Check your work.

Activity D - *Collecting Forms*
1. Collect as many kinds of forms as you can find.
2. How are they alike?
3. How are they different?
4. List the things you need to know to fill them out properly.

Activity E - *Make A Form*
1. Think of a product you want to sell.
2. Create an order form for your product.
    or
1. Think of a job you would like.
2. Create an application form for that job.

Evaluation: Activity A - Number coding on the back of vocabulary and definition cards.
Activities B and C - Separate answer keys.
Activities D and E - Teacher correction.

Area: Reading

Purpose: To reinforce students' ability to follow directions

Suggested Grade Levels: K-8

Objectives: Students will follow directions in order to repair classroom instructional materials such as learning center activities and games.

Materials:

- Construction materials such as tape, scissors, construction paper, magic markers, and folders
- Damaged instructional materials such as games and center activities
- Directions clipped to each activity to be repaired describing what is to be done to repair it
- Two large boxes - one labeled "In" and one labeled "Out"

Directions

Activity A - *Fix It!*

1. Select one of the activities to be repaired.
2. Read the directions which are clipped to the material.
3. "Fix It!"
4. Put the repaired activity in the "Out" box.

Evaluation: Teacher evaluation. The teacher checks the material for satisfactory "repair" and writes a note to the students indicating that the work is complete.

Area: Mathematics

Note: •This center can be used to study the numbers 1-20.

•The center can be modified to include fewer activities.

•More than one numeral could be presented at a time.

•Have students practice each activity in a small group before doing them independently.

Purpose: To reinforce concepts about the numeral seven (or, a specific numeral)

Suggested Grade Levels: K-2

Objectives: Students will make sets of seven.*

Students will complete number sentences whose sum is seven.*

Students will complete number sentences involving subtracting numbers from seven.*

Students will write number sentences about seven.*

Materials: *For Activity A:*

•Large cards showing complete number sentences involving seven* on the front and a picture of the sets making seven* on the back, for example:

$$1+6=7$$

•Devices for making sets such as:

large wooden beads and laces	checkers
chalk and small chalkboards	buttons
pegs and pegboards	popsicle sticks
flannel figures and magnetic boards	

For Activity B:

•chart listing number sentences about seven*

•cards showing incomplete number sentences with answers on the back

For Activity C:

•pocket cards with number sentences on the pockets and answers on the tab cards

For Activity D:
- dittoed, workbook, or teacher-constructed page with incomplete number sentences inserted in acetate sheet
- grease pencil • facial tissue • pen

For Activity E:
- pencil • paper

Directions

Activity A - *Make Seven**
1. Look at the cards that show how to make seven.*
2. Make sets of seven to go with the number sentence on each card. Make the sets with

    beads   flannelboard
    pegboards   checkers
    magnetic board

Activity B - *Finish the Number Sentences*
1. Look at the number sentences in the box.
2. Finish each number sentence. Use the counters to help you.
3. Look on the back of the card to check your work.

Activity C - *Use the Pocket Cards*
1. Look at the pocket cards in the box.
2. Find the little card that fits in each pocket.
3. Look on the back of the pocket card to check your work.
4. If you have trouble, use the counters to help you.

Activity D - *Test Yourself*
1. Get a worksheet, grease pencil and tissue.
2. Finish the number sentences.
3. Check your work.
4. If you have trouble, use the counters to help you.

Activity E - *Make a Book About Seven**
1. Make a book about seven.*
2. Put a page in your book for each number sentence about seven that is listed on the chart.
3. Make sets to go with each number sentence.
   - draw pictures
   - cut out pictures
   - glue objects to the pages
4. Put your book in the folder.

Evaluation: Activity A - teacher observation.
    Activities B and C - self-check, answers on backs of cards.
    Activity D - self-check, separate answer keys.
    Activity E - teacher correction.

*Or any number, 1-20

Area: Mathematics

Purpose: To reinforce students' ability to place numbers in sequential (serial) order

Suggested Grade Levels: 1-2

Objectives: Students will identify the numeral or numerals which are missing from a set of numbers presented in consecutive order.

Materials: paper and pencil

For Activity A:

• Sets of "bone" base cards in envelopes kept in a box. Examples of sets include:

Set 1: One numeral missing

Set 2: Two numerals missing

Set 3: More than two numerals missing

Set 4: Counting by 2's - one numeral missing

Set 5: Counting by 5's - one numeral missing

Set 6: Counting by 10's - one numeral missing

• Insert cards appropriate for "bone" base cards. A slit should be cut in each card.

• Large manila folders for each set of cards

For Activity B:

• Dittoed worksheets containing items similar to those in the sample.

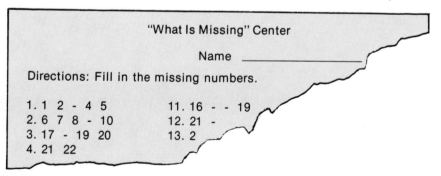

"What Is Missing" Center

Name _____

Directions: Fill in the missing numbers.

1. 1 2 - 4 5
2. 6 7 8 - 10
3. 17 - 19 20
4. 21 22

11. 16 - - 19
12. 21 -
13. 2

Directions

Activity A - *What Numeral Is Missing?*

1. Get an envelope from the box.
2. Look at the numerals on each card in the envelope.
3. What numeral is missing?
4. Put the missing numeral in the pocket.
5. Check your work.

Activity B - *Fill in the Missing Numbers*

1. Get a worksheet.
2. Read each item carefully.
3. Fill in the missing numbers.
4. Check your work.
   Place your work in the folder.

C - *You Write the Problems*

   a sheet of paper and a pencil.
   ld your paper into eight blocks.
3. Write a "What Is Missing" problem in each block.
4. Make an answer key.

Note: Include as many activities as appropriate for the group.

Evaluation: Activity A - self-check, answers on backs of cards.
   Activity B - self-check, separate answer key.
   Activity C - teacher correction.

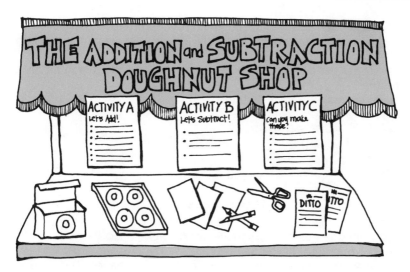

Area: Mathematics

Purpose: To reinforce basic number facts

Suggested Grade Levels: 1-2

Objectives: Students will supply the missing numerals in number sentences with sums less than 20.

Students will supply the missing numerals in number sentences involving subtraction from numbers less than 20.

Materials: *For Activity A:*

- "Doughnuts" about 3 inches in diameter. (The doughnuts can be decorated by students.)
- Doughnut box obtained from a doughnut shop, or a box decorated to resemble one.

For Activities A and B:

- 2 long flat boxes to be used for "trays"

For Activity C:

- construction paper
- ditto with number sentences to be completed
- scissors
- pencil
- crayons

Introduction:

This center will help you practice your addition and subtraction facts.

Directions

Activity A - *Let's Add!*

1. Work with a partner.
2. Get the tray of addition doughnuts.
3. Give your partner the doughnut box.

4. Read the number sentence on each doughnut to your partner.
5. If your partner answers it correctly, he or she can put the doughnut in the box.
6. If your partner does not answer it correctly, put the doughnut back on the tray.
7. Trade places with your partner.

Activity B - *Let's Subtract*

1. Work with a partner.
2. Get the tray of subtraction doughnuts.
3. Follow the directions that you used in Activity A.

Activity C - *Can You Make These?*

1. Get a worksheet.
2. Complete the number sentences on the worksheet.
3. Check your work. If you had trouble, do the problem again.
4. Make twelve "doughnuts" from construction paper. Decorate each doughnut.
5. Cut the number sentences from the worksheet. Paste one on each doughnut.
6. Use your doughnuts for practice.

Evaluation: Activities A and B - self-check, answers on backs of doughnuts.
Activity C - teacher correction.

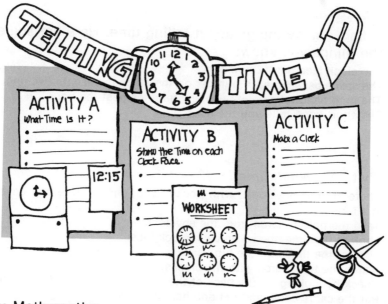

Area: Mathematics

Purpose: To reinforce concepts related to telling time

Suggested Grade Levels: 2-3

Objectives: Students will tell the time.

Students will draw hands on clock faces to show specific times.

Students will construct a clock.

Materials: *For Activity A:*

•Pocket cards with clock faces showing specific times and tab cards showing that time.
•Set one: Twelve pocket cards showing hours.
•Set two: Twelve pocket cards showing thirty minutes past the hour.
•Set three: Fifteen pocket cards showing fifteen and forty-five minutes past the hour.
•Set four: Fifteen pocket cards showing multiples of five minutes past the hour.
•Set five: Fifteen pocket cards showing a variety of numbers of minutes past the hour.

Note: To make pocket cards efficiently, run clock faces off on a ditto and draw hands after gluing the clock face to the pocket card.

For Activity B:

•dittos with clock faces without hands

For Activity C:

•paper plates
•construction paper

•pencils
•scissors

For All Activities:

•paper fasteners

Introduction:

You know many things about telling time. Here are some of the things you know:

1. The clock face has 12 numbers.
2. The space between each number on the clock represents five minutes.
3. The long hand tells you how many minutes past the hour it is.
4. The short hand tells you the hour.

Directions

Activity A - *What Time Is It?*

1. There are five envelopes with pocket cards inside. Use one envelope at a time.
2. Take the pocket cards from the envelope.
3. Look at the time shown on each clock face.
4. Look at the times on the tab cards.
5. Match the time cards with the clocks.
6. Check by looking on the back of the pocket card.
7. Put the cards back and get another envelope.

Activity B - *Show the Time on Each Clock Face*

1. Get a worksheet.
2. Look at the time listed below each clock face.
3. Draw hands on each clock face to show the time.
4. Check your work by looking at the answer key.

Activity C - *Make a Clock*

1. Get these materials:

paper plate	paper fastener
scissors	small piece of construction paper
pencil	

2. Study the clock.
3. Put numerals on your clock.
4. Use small lines to show the minutes between numbers.
5. Make a long hand and a short hand for your clock.
6. Attach them to your clock with a paper fastener.
7. Make a list of times.
8. Give your clock and the list of times to a friend. Can your friend show the times?

Evaluation: Activity A - self-check, answers on backs of pocket cards.
Activity B - self-check, separate answer keys or teacher correction.
Activity C - teacher observation.

Area: Mathematics

Purpose: To reinforce and review subtraction skills

Suggested Grade Levels: 4-5

Objectives: Students will solve word problems involving subtraction of four digit numbers with renaming.

Materials: paper and pencil

For Activities A and B:

•Used car ads from the local newspaper

For Activity A:

•A set of question cards* (Set A) with questions such as these:
"Which car costs more - the 1973 Dodge Dart or the 1972 Plymouth Valiant? How much more?"
"Which car costs least - the 1975 Ford Mustang, the 1974 Ford Maverick, or the 1975 Dodge Charger?"
*Cards might be cut in the shape of cars for added student interest.

For Activity B:

•A set of question cards (Set B) such as these:
John has saved $750 for a car. How much more does he need to buy the 1969 VW?
Mr. Smith paid $3561 for the 1973 Impala which he is now selling for $1200. How much less will he get for the car than he originally paid?

Directions

Activity A - *Which Costs More?*

1. Read the questions in Set A.
2. Refer to the used car ads to get the information you need to answer the questions.
3. Write your answers on an answer sheet.
4. Check your work.

Activity B - *Find the Difference*

1. Read the questions in Set B.
2. Refer to the used car ads to get any information you might need to answer the questions.
3. Write your answers on an answer sheet.
4. Check your work.

Activity C - *Develop Some Problems*

1. Find some used car ads in the newspaper.
2. Use the information from the ads to write some problems for your friends to answer.
3. Include an answer key.
4. Put your finished project in the project folder.

Evaluation: Activities A and B - self-check, separate answer key, or answers on the backs of the cards.

Activity C - teacher evaluation.

Area: Mathematics

Purpose: To reinforce concepts and skills related to metric measurement.

Suggested Grade Levels: 2-4

Objectives: Students will measure items with a metric ruler. Students will sort items according to size.

Materials: paper and pencil

For Activity A:

"Treasure Box"
- old jewelry   • old bottles   • ribbon
- small pieces of fabric such as velvet, brocade, or satin
- Treasure Measure Record Sheets
- metric ruler
- envelopes
- "gold" coins made from shiny gold paper or yellow construction paper.

Directions

Introduction:

You have just found a buried treasure! When you open the treasure box you find this note:

> If you find this treasure take everything less than 15 cm out of the box. You must put everything more than 15 cm long back in the box!

You get one piece of gold for each item less than 15 cm long.

You get two pieces of gold for each item more than 15 cm long.

Find out how much gold you can get!

MEASURE CAREFULLY!!!

The Metric Pirate

Activity A - *Finding Gold*

1. Measure each item in the treasure box.
2. Write the length of each item on the Treasure Measure Record.
3. Decide how much gold you get.
4. Check your work.
5. If you are right, exchange your record card for gold.

Activity B - *A Sizable Treasure List*

1. List all the items in the Treasure Box according to size, from the smallest to the largest.
2. Check your answers with the key.

Activity C - *Making Treasure Measures*

1. Draw 6 items for a "Treasure Measure Box"
   - a string of pearls 15 cm long
   - a glass bottle 10 cm long
   - a diamond 5 cm long
   - a golden coin 20 cm in diameter
   - a silver knife 30 cm long
   - a silver mug 6 cm high
2. Carefully cut out the treasures.
3. Put them in an envelope decorated like a Treasure Box.
4. Place your Treasure Box in the folder.

Activity D - *Make Your Own Treasure Measure Box*

1. Draw as many items as you would like for a Treasure Measure Box.
2. Measure each item carefully and make an answer key.
3. Put the treasures in a box or envelope.
4. Decorate the box or envelope like a Treasure Box.
5. Write directions.
6. Have a friend measure your treasures.
7. Place this Treasure Measure Box in the folder.

Evaluation: Activities A and B - self-check, answers on separate answer key.
Activities C and D - teacher correction.

Area: Mathematics

Purpose: To reinforce division skills

Suggested Grade Levels: 4-5

Objectives: Students will solve word problems involving multiplication and division.

Materials: •paper •pencil

For Activity A:

•Sets of activity cards containing portions of ads from grocery stores and questions based on those ads.

Sample Activity Card

> orange juice - 35¢/can, or 3 cans 99¢
> pears - 60¢/lb., or 2 lbs. for $1.00
> ground meat - 75¢/lb., or 5 lbs. for $3.25
> candy bars - 10¢ each, or 5 bars for 45¢

SUPER SAVER SPECIALS!
1. How much do you save per can if you buy 3 cans of orange juice for 99¢?
2. How much do you save per pound if you buy 5 lbs. of hamburger for $3.25?
3. How much would three candy bars cost if bought singly?

Note: The ads can be teacher made, or can be clipped from the newspaper.

For Activity B:

•Newspapers containing grocery store ads.

Directions

Activity A - *Solving Problems*

1 Read the questions on the activity cards.
2. Use the worksheets to solve the problems.
3. Check your work.

Activity B - *Writing Problems*

1. Find a grocery ad in one of the newspapers.
2. Write five problems about the information in the grocery ad.
3. Make an answer key.
4. Put your problem cards and answer key in the folder.

Evaluation: Activity A, self-check, answers on backs of cards.
Activity B, teacher correction.

Area: Mathematics

Purpose: To reinforce skills in working with decimals

Suggested Grade Levels: 5-7

Objectives: Students will add and subtract decimals to solve problems.

Students will compute decimals from fractional equivalents.

Materials: paper and pencil

For Activity A:

•Chart showing names of baseball players and their batting averages. (The chart could be teacher made, or could be clipped from the sports section of the newspaper during baseball season.)

Note: Students might help collect the averages and make the charts.

For Activity B:

•Answer sheets for recording answers to problems on the activity cards. (Students may wish to bring pictures of their favorite baseball players.)

•Chart giving information about number of times at bat and number of hits for each player. Examples of batting average computations are included.

•Activity cards with questions such as these:
  1. Who has the highest batting average?
  2. How much higher is Jones' batting average than Smith's?
  3. Whose batting average is highest...Barnes', Snyder's, or Greene's?
  4. How much higher is his average than those of the other two?

5. How much higher would Greene's batting average have to be in order to be as high as Brown's?
6. How much less than 1.000 is Sander's batting average?

Note: Develop problems at varying levels of difficulty. Put easier problems on one card, harder problems on other cards.

Directions

Activity A - *Looking at the Averages*

1. Read the information about the team's batting averages on the chart.
2. Solve the problems on the Activity Cards. Use the paper at the center to do your computations.
3. List your answers on the answer sheet.
4. Check your work.

Activity B - *Finding the Averages*

1. Using the information on chart B, find (compute) the batting averages for each of the players. Use the example on the chart to help you. (Note: Computing batting averages is done by dividing the number of times at bat by the number of hits.)
2. Record your answers on an answer sheet.
3. Check your work.

Evaluation: Activities A and B - self-check, separate answer keys.

Area: Science

Purpose: To reinforce a unit on animal habitats

Suggested Grade Levels: 1-2

Objectives: Students will describe how the animals find or make their homes.

Students will associate animals with their homes.

Materials: •crayons •paper •pencil

•cut-out pictures of animals familiar to students

jungle animals (e.g., lions, tigers)
forest animals (e.g., squirrels, deer)
farm animals (e.g., cows, pigs)
water animals (e.g., beavers, muskrats)

For Activity A:

•cans or boxes which have been decorated and labeled

jungle   farm
forest   water

For Activity B:

•"animal homes" spinner listing four general types of homes

For Activity C:

•4 animal spinners (one for each habitat area) picturing animals who live in that area

Note:

•words could be substituted for pictures
•students can help to make the spinners by finding pictures of animals

Directions

Activity A: *Where Do They Live?*

1. Look at the animal pictures.
2. Put the animal pictures in the cans that show where they live.
3. Check your work.

Activity B: *Who Lives Here?*

1. Spin the arrow on the Animal Homes Spinner.
2. Name the place where the arrow stops.
3. Name as many animals as you can who live in that place.
4. Draw a picture of these animals.
(optional)
5. Write the animal names under their pictures.
6. Put your name on the paper and put it in the folder.

Activity C: *Describe Their Homes*

1. Choose one of the animal spinners.
2. Name the animal on which the spinner stops.
3. Draw a picture of that animal in or beside its home.
4. Tell how the animal finds or makes this home.

Evaluation: Activity A - self-check, answers on backs of cans or separate answer keys.

Activities B and C - self-check, answers on backs of spinners.

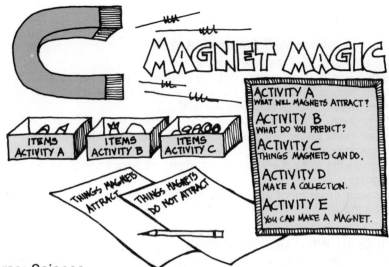

Area: Science

Purpose: To reinforce a unit on magnets

Suggested Grade Levels: 1-3

Objectives: Students will determine which items are attracted by magnets and which are not.

Students will record their findings.

Materials: *For Activities A and B:*

• bar magnets   • horseshoe magnets

• Items which are not attracted by magnets such as cloth, paper, plastic toys, crayons, markers. (Mix items which are and are not attracted by magnets.) Put both types of items in each of two boxes. Mark one box "A" and the other box "B".

• Record Keeping Sheet

    Things Magnets Attract
    Things Magnets Do Not Attract

For Activity B:

• Items which are not attracted by magnets such as cloth, paper, plastic toys, crayons, markers. (Mix items which are and are not attracted by magnets.) Put both types of items in each of two boxes. Mark one box "A" and the other box "B".

• Prediction Sheet

    Things I Think Magnets Will Attract
    Things I Think Magnets Will Not Attract

For Activity C:

• sheets of paper

• piece of glass

• items which are attracted by magnets such as paper clips, nails, tacks, pins, scissors...(items containing iron). Place in a box marked "C".

Directions

Activity A: *What Will Magnets Attract?*

1. Get a magnet and the box of items marked "A".
2. Taking one item at a time, put the magnet close to each item.
3. If the item is attracted by the magnet, list or draw it on your record sheet under "Things Magnets Attract".
4. If the item is not attracted by the magnet, list or draw it on your record sheet under "Things Magnets Do Not Attract".
5. Check your work with the answer key.
6. What seems to be the same about the items which are attracted by the magnet?
7. Try your experiment again with a different magnet. Did you find the same thing?

Activity B: *What Do You Predict?*

1. Get "Box B", a magnet, and a prediction sheet. Look carefully at each item in Box "B".
2. If you think it will be attracted by the magnet, list or draw it on your prediction sheet under "Things I Think Magnets Will Attract".
3. If you think it will not be attracted by the magnet, list or draw it on your prediction sheet under "Things I Think Magnets Will Not Attract".
4. Now put the magnet close to each item. Were your predictions correct? If not, change your prediction sheet.
5. Check your work with the answer key.

Introduction: Sometimes magnets pick up things even though those things are covered with something else.

Activity C: *Things Magnets Can Do*

1. Take the items from Box C. What is alike about these items?
2. Now cover each with paper. Does the magnet still attract it?
3. Cover each item with glass. Does the magnet still attract it?
4. Write a sentence telling what you discovered.
5. Put your sentence in the folder.

Activity D: *Make A Collection*

1. Make a collection of things magnets attract. Try each item with a magnet to be sure you are right.
2. Label your collection.
3. Show your collection to your teacher.

Activity E: *You Can Make A Magnet!*

1. Get a nail and a magnet.
2. Rub the nail with the magnet. Use only one pole of the magnet and rub the nail many times in the same direction.
3. See how many paper clips or pins you can pick up with your magnet.

4. Wait 5 minutes, see how many paper clips or pins you can pick up with your magnet.
5. Write what happened.
6. Put your answer in the folder.

Evaluation: Activities A and B - separate answer keys.
Activities C, D and E - teacher correction.

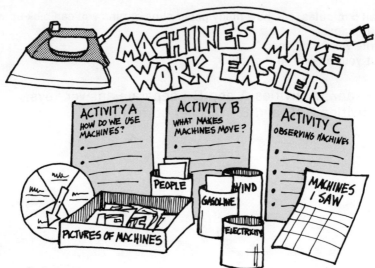

Area: Science

Purpose: To reinforce a unit on machines

Suggested Grade Levels: 1-3

Objectives: Students will classify machines into those which cut things, those which move things, those for travel, and those which help make work easier.

Students will describe what makes machines move.

Students will observe the use of machines and keep records of their observations.

Materials: *For Activity A:*

•Large spinner with four sections: machines that cut things, machines that move things, machines we can ride in, machines that make work easy. Some items may appear more than once.

For Activities A and B: paper and pencil

•Pictures of
  -machines that cut things (e.g., saw, scissors, can opener, drill, meat slicer)
  -machines that can move things (e.g., wagon, truck, train, bulldozer, pulley)
  -machines we can ride in (e.g., bus, car, ferris wheel, merry-go-round, airplane, bike, ship)
  -machines that make work easy (e.g., lawn mower, mixer, vacuum cleaner, washing machine)

•Large juice cans with these labels:
  -Electricity makes these machines work.
  -Gasoline makes these machines work.
  -People make these machines work.
  -Water makes these machines work.

Note: it is important to discuss the relationship between humans using or monitoring machines.

• Record sheets

| Machines I Saw | | Name _____ |
| | | Date |

Machine	What Made It Move *(electricity, gasoline,* *people, wind, water)*	How It Helped *(work, ride, travel)*

Summary

I saw _____machines.

Gasoline made _____machines move.

Electricity made_____machines move.

Wind made _____machines move.

Water made_____machines move.

People made _____machines move.

I saw _____different kinds of machines that moved things.

I saw _____different kinds of machines that cut things.

I saw _____different kinds of things for travel.

I saw _____different kinds of things to help make work easier.

Introduction:

We learned that machines are used to help us move things, to help us cut things, to help us do many kinds of work, and to help us travel.

Directions

Activity A: *How Do We Use Machines?*

1. Look at the pictures in the box.
2. Read the titles on the spinner.
3. Spin the spinner. Read the title on which the spinner stops.
4. Find as many pictures as you can that go with that title.
5. Check your work.

Introduction: We learned that electricity, gasoline, people, wind, and water can make machines move.

Activity B: *What Makes Machines Move?*

1. Look at the pictures.
2. Think about what makes the machines in the pictures work.
3. Put the pictures in the cans which tell what makes the machines move.
4. Check your work.

Activity C: *Observing Machines*

1. Look for all kinds of machines wherever you go for the next five days.
2. Keep a record of the machines you saw. Use the sheet called "Machines I Saw" to list them. The record sheet might include the following information:
    -when you saw it
    -what it was
    -how it helped do work
    -what made it move
3. Make a summary of the information which you have collected.
4. Put your record sheet and summary in the folder.

Evaluation: Activity A - self-check, answers written on back of spinner.

Activity B - self-check, answers written on backs of cans or separate answer key.

Activity C - teacher and student discussion, teacher evaluation.

EXPLORING EVAPORATION

Area: Science

Purpose: To reinforce a unit on evaporation

Suggested Grade Levels: 2-4

Objectives: Students will conduct experiments which show that under certain conditions water evaporates quicker than under other conditions.

Students will describe and record their findings.

Materials: paper and pencil
- tall glasses
- small chalkboards
- sponges
- crayons
- cloths
- plastic bags
- shallow pans
- thumbtacks

Introduction:

Evaporation

1. Water evaporates.
2. When water evaporates, it goes into the air.
3. We cannot see the water which has evaporated.
4. Wind speeds the process of water evaporation.
5. Sun speeds the process of water evaporation.

Now try these experiments:

Experiment I:

1. Work with a partner.
2. Get these materials:
   cloths (or paper towels)
   2 plastic bags
   thumbtacks
3. Make one cloth wet.

4. Put each cloth into a plastic bag and tie each bag shut.
5. Tack each bag to the bulletin board.
6. Watch the bags for several days.
7. What happens to the bag with the wet cloth inside?
8. Open each bag. Keep them both hanging on the bulletin board.
9. Watch the bags for several days.
10. What happens to the wet cloth? What happens to the drops of water on the inside of the bag?
11. List what you did in your experiment. Illustrate and discuss what happened at each step.

Experiment II:

1. Work with a partner.
2. Get these materials:
   • sponge
   • water
   • paper fan
   • paper
   • 2 small chalkboards
3. Make a large wet circle on each chalkboard with the sponge.
4. Fan the one wet spot. Do not fan the other.
5. Which dries more quickly? Why?
6. Describe your experiment. Include what you did at each step and why you did it.

Experiment III:

1. Work with a partner.
2. Get these materials:
   • paper
   • tape
   • 3 shallow containers
   • water
   • 3 bottles
   • measuring cup
3. Tape your name on each container.
4. Put ½ cup of water in each container and each bottle. Measure carefully!
5. Place a bottle and a container in each of these three places
   1. near the heater
   2. near a window
   3. in a dark corner
6. Study your containers each day.
7. What happens to the water in the containers?
8. From which containers does the water evaporate most rapidly? Most slowly?
9. What can you conclude about your experiments?
10. Describe your experiment. Include what you did at each step and why you did it.

Evaluation: Teacher-student discussion groups.
Teacher-correction of student notes.

Area: Science

Purpose: To reinforce a unit on planets

Suggested Grade Levels: 3-4

Objectives: Students will associate planets with their characteristics.

Students will make a model of the solar system.

Students will describe the sun as the chief source of light for the moon and planets of the solar system.

Materials: •A large chart or picture of the solar system

For Activity A:

•Description cards of the planets with characteristics listed on the front and the name of the planet on the back.

MERCURY	1. This planet is nearest the sun. It is hotter there than on any other planet. It is the smallest planet.
PLUTO	2. This planet gets very little light from the sun. It is farthest from the sun. It is the coldest planet.
EARTH	3. This planet is covered with plants and animals. It is 93 million miles from the Sun. This planet is more than half covered with water.
MARS	4. This planet is most like the Earth. It has a thin layer of atmosphere. It has white polar caps around its north and south poles. Some people think there may be plants there. It has seasons. There is not much water there.
VENUS	5. Next to the sun and moon, this is the brightest light we see in the sky. It is nearest the Earth and about the same size. It is much, much hotter than the Earth. A spacecraft named Mariner II went there.
JUPITER	6. This is the largest planet. It has an atmosphere of poisonous gases. It has no oxygen or water. It has twelve moons.

SATURN	7. This planet has rings which circle it. It has nine moons. It has no water or oxygen.
URANUS	8. This planet is very cold. It has an atmosphere of poisonous gases. It takes 84 of our years for it to revolve around the sun. It has 5 moons.
NEPTUNE	9. This planet is cold. It takes about 165 of our years for it to travel once around the sun. It has two moons.

For Activity B:

• Game cards with statements such as
 1. Name the hottest planet.
 2. Name the planet with rings.
 3. Name the planet similar in size to Earth.
 4. Tell two things about Venus.
 5. What is atmosphere?

   Number each card. Assign each card a number of points.
   A correct answer allows the player to move that number of spaces.

• Answer key for the cards.
• Game board
• Playing pieces in the form of space ships

For Activity C:

• construction paper
• glue
• scissors
• yarn

Introduction: Pretend you are taking travelers on a "guided tour" of the solar system. What would you tell visitors at each stop?

Directions

Activity A: *Find the Planet*

1. Read the descriptions of the planets on the cards.
2. Place each card on the planet which it describes.
3. Check your work.

Activity B: *Play the Space Race Game*

1. Play with a partner.
2. Draw a card. Read the question, and give an answer.
3. Ask your partner to check the answer key to see if you are right.
4. If you are right, move your space ship the number of spaces indicated on the card.
5. If you are wrong, stay where you are.
6. The next player takes a turn.
7. The person who reaches "Splash Down" first is the winner.

Activity C: *Make a Model of the Solar System*

1. Study the information about the solar system in your textbook and other materials at the center.
2. Sketch a design for your model of the solar system.
3. Use construction paper, yarn, glue, and fabric to make your model.
4. Label each planet and give a one sentence description of it.
5. Show in your model the relationship of each planet to the sun.
6. Discuss your model with your teacher.

Evaluation: Activity A - self-check, answers on backs of cards.
Activity B - self-check, answer key.
Activity C - teacher correction.

Area: Science / Reading

Purpose: To reinforce a unit interpreting nutrition information from food labels.

Suggested Grade Levels: 6-8

Objectives: Students will locate nutrition information on food labels.

Students will use information from food labels to solve nutrition problems and plan menus.

Materials: paper and pencil

For Activity A:

Question cards which require students to locate nutrition information on food labels that are attached to the cards.

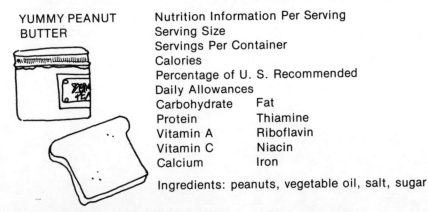

YUMMY PEANUT BUTTER

Nutrition Information Per Serving
Serving Size
Servings Per Container
Calories
Percentage of U. S. Recommended Daily Allowances

Carbohydrate	Fat
Protein	Thiamine
Vitamin A	Riboflavin
Vitamin C	Niacin
Calcium	Iron

Ingredients: peanuts, vegetable oil, salt, sugar

1. How large is a serving size?
2. How many servings are in this jar?
3. How many calories are in each serving of peanut butter?

4. What percentage of the U.S. Recommended Daily Allowances of these nutrients is found in one serving?

Protein_____   Niacin_____
Vitamin A_____   Calcium_____
Vitamin C_____

5. What ingredients are found in this peanut butter?

For Activity B:

•Question cards which require students to compare and contrast the nutrition information found on several food labels that are attached to the cards.

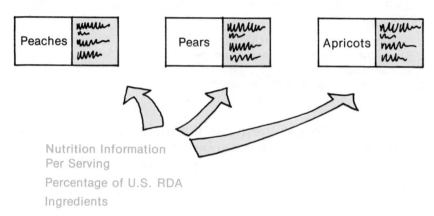

Peaches   Pears   Apricots

Nutrition Information
Per Serving

Percentage of U.S. RDA

Ingredients

1. What is the serving size of each?
2. Which has the most calories per serving size?
3. Which has more Vitamin C per serving size?
4. Which has more grams of carbohydrate per serving size?
5. Which ingredients are found in each of the foods?

For Activity C:

•A chart with labels from a variety of foods that might be combined for a meal: tuna, peas, peaches, rolls, candy bar, and milk.
•Question cards which require students to solve problems.

Sally had these things for lunch:
½ cup of tuna   1 roll
½ cup of peas   1 candy bar
½ cup of peaches   1 cup of milk

How much of the MDR of each of these nutrients has she had? How much more does she need to get from breakfast and dinner?

	Have	Need		Have	Need
Calcium	_____	_____	Niacin	_____	_____
Vitamin A	_____	_____	Calcium	_____	_____
Vitamin C	_____	_____	Riboflavin	_____	_____

How many calories did she have for lunch?
Plan a breakfast and dinner for her which would provide the nutrients
she needs.

Directions

Introduction: We have learned that food labels provide
nutrition information to help us eat wisely. This activity
will help you find that information.

Activity A: *What Nutrition Information Does a Food Label Tell You?*
1. Read the questions on each card.
2. Study the nutrition information on the labels.
3. Answer each question.
4. Check your work with the answer key.

Introduction: To get the most nutrition from the food we
buy, we should compare nutrition information on food
labels. This activity will help you make comparisons.

Activity B: *How Can Nutrition Information Give Us Information About What to Eat?*
1. Read the questions on each card.
2. Study the nutrition information on the labels.
3. Answer the questions.
4. Check your work with the answer key.

Introduction: Nutrition information helps us plan meals. This
activity will help you with meal planning.

Activity C: *Can You Plan a Balanced Meal?*
1. Read the questions on each card.
2. Use the nutrition information on the food labels found on the chart to
answer the questions.
3. Check your work with the answer key.

Introduction: Are you getting the nutrition you need from your
meals? This activity will help you find out.

Activity D: *You Are What You Eat*
1. List everything you eat for one day.
2. Find out as much as you can about the nutrition content of what
you have eaten.
3. For which nutrients did you have the MDR?
   For which nutrients did you have less than the MDR?

4. Write a summary of what you ate, the nutrition information about those foods, and what you needed to meet the MDR.
5. Put your summary in the folder.

Evaluation: Activities A, B and C - self-check, separate answer keys.
Activity D - teacher correction.

Area: Social Studies

Purpose: To reinforce a unit on friends

Suggested Grade Levels: 1-2

Objectives: Students will identify many types of friends one might have.

Students will describe things they can do to make new friends.

Students will identify ways to solve problems which they may encounter with their friends.

Materials: •paper   •crayons

For Activity A:

•pictures of many kinds of friends

children	adults	relatives
teenagers	pets	teacher

neighborhood helpers (doctor, police officer)

For Activity B:

•chart that students can make which gives tips for making friends
•cards with "Do's" and "Don'ts" for making friends

For Activity C:

•problem cards (student-made)
•puppets

Directions

Activity A - *Your Friends*

1. Look at the pictures of friends we might have.
2. Draw a picture of friends you have.
3. Write their names under their pictures if you can.

4. Put your pictures in the folder.

Activity B - *How to Make New Friends*

1. How can we make new friends?
2. Read the chart you wrote.
3. Put the cards in the cans that say "Do" and "Don't".

Activity C - *When Friends Have Problems*

1. Sometimes friends have problems.
2. Study the problem shown on each card.
3. Think of a way to solve the problem.
4. Have the puppets show the way to solve the problem.

Evaluation: Activities A-C, teacher and group discussion.

Area: Social Studies

Purpose: To reinforce a unit on transportation

Suggested Grade Levels: 1-2

Objectives: Students will identify types of transportation.
Students will identify which types of transportation are best suited for specific purposes.
Students will be able to compare and contrast types of transportation.

Materials: paper and pencil

For Activity A:

•Travel Mat
A large scene drawn on fabric* (with magic marker) showing sky, water, roads, and railroad tracks
*construction paper or tagboard could be used, if preferred

•word cards listing ways we can travel

water	air	rails	roads

•picture/word cards* for types of transportation such as

trains	motorcycles
trucks	jets
cars	airplanes
boats	helicopters
ships	bikes
ocean liners	person walking

*toy items could be substituted

For Activity B:
•spinner showing types of transportation
For Activity C:
•two cubes with pictures showing means of transportation on each side
  of each cube
•problem cards

Mr. Smith wants to take cows to his new farm.	Mr. Adams must take big logs to the mill.	Cindy wants to take a vacation in England.

•boxes labeled

sky	water	roads	railroads	land

Introduction

People can go from place to place in many ways. They can travel on land, on water, or in the air.

Directions

Activity A - *The Ways and Hows of Travel*

1. Open the Travel Mat and put it on the table.
2. Put the word cards on the places that show how we can travel.
3. Get the picture cards that show how we can travel.
4. Put the pictures of ways to travel on the Travel Mat where they belong.
5. Check your work.

Activity B - *Types of Travel*

1. Spin the spinner.
2. Name the picture where the spinner stops.
3. Tell these things about the picture:
   •Where would it travel?
   •Who could use it?
   •What could it carry?
4. Look on the back to check your work.

Activity C - *Ways to Travel*

1. Roll both cubes.
2. Name the picture on each.
3. Make two lists about the pictures:
   •How are they alike?
   •How are they different?
4. Think about things like this in making your lists:
   •How big are they?
   Where do they travel?
   •What do they carry?
   •How much does it cost to use them?
5. Put your lists in the folder.

Activity D - *Why People Travel*

1. Why do people travel? List as many reasons as you can why people travel.
2. Compare your list with the list in the folder.
3. Each of the problem cards tells about a person who needs to travel. Decide which way that person can choose to travel.
4. Put the card in the box with that label.
5. Check your work.

Activity E - *Your Way to Travel*

1. Choose a way that you like to travel.
2. Make a book about it.
   For example, if you write your book about trucks, you might want to include:
   a. pictures of different kinds of trucks
   b. where they can travel
   c. what they can carry.
3. Share your book with the class.

Evaluation: Activity A, self-check, separate answer key.
Activity B, group discussion.
Activity C, teacher-correction and/or group discussion.
Activity D, self-check, answers on backs of boxes.
Activity E, teacher correction.

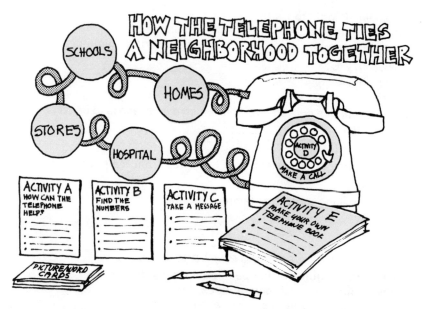

Area: Social Studies

Purpose: To reinforce a unit on using the telephone for communication within the neighborhood

Suggested Grade Levels: 1-3

Objectives: Students will describe how the telephone can be used for communication within a neighborhood.

Students will learn how to find information in the neighborhood phone book.

Students will practice making calls within their neighborhood.

Students will practice taking messages from calls made by people in their neighborhood.

Materials: paper and pencil

Activity A:

•Picture/word cards showing persons representing various occupations and situations within a neighborhood. For example.

department store salesperson	fire fighter
secretary	taxi driver
grocery clerk	child
doctor	airline clerk
teacher	garage mechanic
pizza shop manager	pet shop clerk

For Activity B:
- Worksheet: People to Call
- white and yellow pages cut from the telephone book
- lists of persons and places whose numbers can be found on the pages

For Activity C:
- paper for messages
- messages
  taped telephone conversations in which a message is to be taken
- tape recorder

For Activity D:
- toy telephones or real telephones borrowed from the phone company

For Activity E:
- paper for making individual telephone books

Directions

Activity A - *How Can the Telephone Help?*
1. Look at the pictures of the people on the cards.
2. Think about what each person does.
3. Think about why you might call each person.
4. Think about the kinds of calls those people would make.
5. Take a worksheet and complete it by filling in the columns.

Name _____

People to Call

Person:_____

Why you might call the person.	What kinds of calls would this person make?
1.	1.
2.	2.
3.	3.
4.	

Activity B - *Find the Numbers*
1. Take a list of persons and places.
2. Pretend you want to make these calls.
3. Read each name or place on the list. Use the white pages from the telephone book to find the telephone numbers of the people. Use the yellow pages of the telephone book to find the numbers of the places.
4. Number your paper. Write the person or place and the telephone number for each on the list.
5. Check your work with the answer key.

Activity C - *Take a Message*

Introduction:

Sometimes you will need to take a message when you answer the telephone. It is important to take messages carefully. You should include these things in your message:
- the name of the caller
- the phone number of the caller
- information which the caller has asked you to give to someone else

1. There are several calls on the tape. Listen to one call at a time.
2. Take a message for each call.
3. Compare your message with the one on the answer key.

Activity D: *Make A Call*

1. Work with a partner. Practice making these calls:
   a. Call a friend to say you will be late,
   b. Call the pizza shop to order a pizza,
   c. Call a theater to see what time a movie begins,
   d. Call the fire department to report a fire.
2. Before you make each call, decide what information you need to give. Do you need to give your name in each example? Your address? What questions will you want to ask?
3. After you have practiced your calls, choose one to put on tape.

Activity E: *Make Your Own Telephone Book*

1. Make your own telephone book.
2. Put the names and places in your telephone directory in alphabetical order.
3. Place your directory in the folder.

Evaluation: Activities A, D and E, teacher-correction.
Activities B and C, self check, separate answer keys.

Area: Social Studies

Purpose: To reinforce a unit on communication by mail

Suggested Grade Levels: 1-3

Objectives: Students will describe how a letter goes from sender to receiver.

Students will describe ways people can make mail service work efficiently.

Students will prepare letters for mailing.

Materials: paper and pencil

For Activity A:

•Sequence cards placed in folder or envelope describing steps in getting mail from sender to receiver

write the letter	address the envelope	put mail in box
mail is picked up by mailperson	mail is delivered to post office	mail is sorted
mail is delivered to home or office		

For Activity B:

•A Zippy Mail Chart

(Chart with tips for addressing envelopes)

1. Write clearly
2. Include your return address
3. Write the person's name and address
4. Include zip code

For Activity C:
- Some incorrectly or incompletely addressed letters and packages (e.g., letters with last name omitted, state omitted, zip code omitted, return address omitted, no stamp, sloppy writing)

For Activity D:
- Blank envelopes

Directions

Activity A - *How Does Mail Get to You?*
1. Read each card in the envelopes.
2. Arrange the cards in order so they tell how mail goes from the sender to the receiver.
3. Check your work.
4. Make a picture to go with each card.

Activity B - *Getting An Envelope Ready to Mail*
1. Study the Zippy Mail Chart.
2. What information should be included on every envelope?
3. Make a list.
4. Compare your list with the answer key.

Activity C - *What's Wrong Here?*
1. Look at the letters in the "dead letter box".
2. Something is wrong with each letter. Decide what is wrong with each letter.
3. Check by looking on the answer key.

Activity D - *Get It Right*
1. Get two envelopes from the box.
2. Address one to a relative and one to a friend following the tips on the Zippy Mail Chart.
3. Draw a stamp here the stamp should be placed.
4. Put your letters in the checking folder.

Evaluation: Activity A, self-check, answers on backs of cards.

Activities B and C, self-check, separate answer keys.

Activity D, teacher correction.

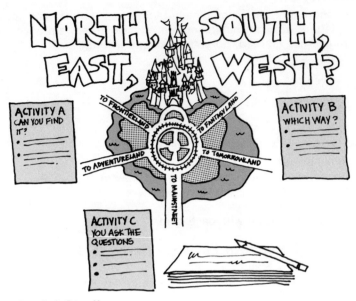

Area: Social Studies

Purpose: To reinforce the skill of using directions in map reading.

Suggested Grade Level: 2-3

Objectives: Students will determine direction traveled by locating places on a map.

Materials: paper and pencil

- Large map of Disney World or Disneyland. (These may be ordered, purchased at a toy store, or can be created by the students themselves.)
- Small statues of Disney characters, or cutouts of these characters which students have made, to be used as an aid while students complete the Activity Cards.

For Activity A:

- A set of activity cards with directions such as these on each:

Set 1
Find Fantasyland on the map of Disneyland. Which of these sentences is true?
Fantasyland is north of Main Street. Fantasyland is south of Main Street.

For Activity A and B:
•large map
•small statues

For Activity B:
•a set of Activity Cards with activities such as these:

Set II

Don and Joan are going from Liberty Square to Fantasyland.
Which way will they travel?

Tom is in Adventureland and Mike is in Tomorrowland.
Who is farther west?

Michelle is in Liberty Square. If she travels directly south,
where will she be?

Directions

Activity A - *Can You Find It?*
1. Use the map to complete the Activity Cards in Set 1.
2. Check your work.

Activity B - *Which Way?*
1. Use the map to complete the Activity Card. , Set II.
2. Check your work.

Activity C - *You Ask the Questions*
1. Make a set of Activity Cards like those in Set I or Set II.
2. Make an answer key.
3. Put your finished project in the project folder.

Evaluation: Activities A and B, Self-check with separate
answer key or answers on back of the cards.
Activity C, Teacher evaluation.

Area: Social Studies

Purpose: To reinforce a unit on Indians

Suggested Grade Levels: 3-4

Objectives: Students will locate and collect information about Indian homes and clothing of long ago.

Students will make models of Indian homes and clothing of long ago.

Materials: paper and pencil

For Activities A-C:

• pictures of Indians of long ago
• books, encyclopedias and magazines containing information about Indians of long ago

For Activity C:

clay	paints
cloth	paste
magic markers	clothespins
mud	scissors

Directions

Activity A - *Learn About Indian Homes*

1. Find information about Indian homes in books, pictures and encyclopedias.

What kinds of homes did Indians have?

What were their homes made of?

How big were their homes?

2. Take notes and make illustrations to help you remember.

Activity B - *Learn About Indian Clothing*
1. Find information about Indian clothing in books, pictures, and encyclopedias.
   What kinds of clothing did Indians wear?
   What was their clothing made of?
   How did they make their clothing?
2. Take notes and make illustrations to help you remember.

Activity C - *Make a Model of an Indian Home*
1. Decide which type of home you would like to make.
2. Make a sketch of the model you plan to build.
3. List the materials you will need.
4. List the steps you will follow in making your model.
5. Gather the materials you need.
6. Make the model.
7. Show the model to your teacher.

Activity D - *Make People for Your Indian Home*
1. Decide how many people you wish to make.
2. Design the clothes you would like them to wear.
3. Use clothespins as a base for your Indian people.
4. Make clothes for your people.
5. Show your "people" to the teacher.

Evaluation: Activities A and B, teacher observation.
   Activities C and D, teacher-student discussion.

Note: This center may be used along with a unit on women in history, or may be used as a means to present instruction. The theme of a similar center could be specific ethnic groups.

Area: Social Studies

Purpose: To introduce (or reinforce) a unit on women who have made significant contributions to America

Suggested Grade Levels: 4-8

Objectives: Students will read about women who have made significant contributions to America.

Students will match names of women with statements of their contributions to America.

Students will use references to prepare an "interview" with a famous American woman.

Materials: *For Activities A and D:*

•References (biographies, textbooks, encyclopedias, dictionaries) containing information about famous American women.

For Activity B:

•Two sets of cards

Set A: containing names of famous American women
Set B: statements of their contributions to the country

For Activity C:

•"Jeopardy" board containing names of American women. Their names have been covered by paper flags.

Introduction:

Many people have helped to make America great! Through the years, women have made numerous significant contributions to their country. This center will help you learn more about some of these women.

Directions

Activity A - *What Did These Woman Do to Make America Great?*

1. Use the references on the shelf to find information about the women whose names are on the bulletin board.
2. Make notes that may help you remember the contributions these women made to their country.

Activity B - *Can You Remember?*

1. Read the names of the women on the cards in Set A.
2. Read the statements about the contributions which these women made to American history in Set B.
3. Match the cards in Set A with those in Set B.
4. Check your work.

Activity C - *Women Who Made America Great: A Quiz*

1. Work with a partner. Use the "Jeopardy" game board.
2. Take turns selecting a box to be uncovered.
3. Select a box (A-1, B-2, etc.).
4. Read the name under the flap.
5. Ask a question about that woman's contribution to America. The answer to the question must be the woman's name. (E.g., Who was a famous woman aviatrix?)

Activity D - *An Interview with a Great American*

1. Select one of the women whose names are on the bulletin board.
2. Using information about this woman from the references on the shelf, create an interview with this person. Include questions such as these:
   Where and when were you born?
   Where did you go to school?
   When did you first become interested in _____?
   What do you think has been your most important contribution to history?
3. Put your completed work in the folder.

Evaluation: Activity A, teacher and group discussion. Activity B, self-check, answers on backs of cards or separate answer key. Activity C, self-check, separate answer key. Activity D, teacher correction.

Possible names to include:

Abigail Adams - Letter Writer	Billie Holiday - Singer
Louisa Mae Alcott - Author, Suffragist	Lucretia Mott - Abolitionist
Clara Barton - Organized American Red Cross	Jeannette Rankin-First Congresswoman
Mary McLeod Bethune -Educator, Administrator	Eleanor Roosevelt - Writer, Social Critic
Elizabeth Blackwell - Physician	Betsy Ross - Seamstress
Isadora Duncan - Dancer	Sacajawea - Guide
Amelia Earhart - Aviatrix	Mary Walker - Civil War Surgeon
Mary Baker Eddy - Religious Leader	Mildred Ella Didrickson Zaharias-Athlete

Chapter 3

Here's How to Use Learning Centers with Exceptional Children

Learning centers offer an excellent means to provide instruction for the exceptional students who are found in every school. The gifted student, the student with specific language disabilities, and the slow learner, all can use learning centers successfully. Whether these students are part of the regular classroom setting, grouped in separate classrooms, or regrouped for part of their school day, learning centers can be used as a basic part of their instructional program.

Teachers usually prefer to extend their basic centers to include activities which are especially appropriate for their exceptional students. However, from time to time, teachers may wish to develop learning centers which are designed specifically for the exceptional students whom they teach.

As you design center activities for the exceptional students in your classroom, you will want to keep in mind both their general learning characteristics and their specific instructional needs. The reference charts presented on the following pages highlight some of the general learning characteristics of exceptional students, and present specific suggestions for planning, developing and using learning centers with these students.

Learning centers cannot and should not be used to replace teacher-directed instruction for exceptional students. Rather, they should be used to supplement, reinforce, and extend instructional concepts presented in teacher-directed settings. It is the well planned combination of teacher-directed activities with learning centers that can make a highly effective, outstanding instructional program for exceptional children.

The Slow Learner

Learning characteristics usually associated with the slow learner include:
- below average ability
- difficulty with conceptualizing, abstracting, problem solving, and identifying relationships
- need to have tasks structured in small, simple, sequential units
- need for many concrete experiences while learning
- need for ample time to learn skills and concepts
- need for much teacher direction
- need for extended readiness activities before learning skills and concepts

Here's how to adapt centers for the slow learner:

Planning

1. Plan short, simple activities for centers rather than longer, more complex tasks.
2. Plan centers which include use of concrete objects and manipulative devices.
3. Plan many centers which reinforce the same skill or concept.
4. Emphasize basic concepts and skills in planning center activities.
5. Plan centers which involve student use of functional reading materials (e.g., telephone books, television guides, catalogues, traffic signs, caution and warning labels).
6. Plan center activities which focus on students' interests as well as on their skill needs.
7. Plan centers which provide students with opportunities to learn communication skills. Among these skills might be:
- using the telephone
- speaking into a tape recorder
- writing short notes
- discussing specific topics with a friend
- making and using puppets
- completing simple order forms

Developing and Using

1. Use audio-visual materials in centers to reduce the amount of reading which is required.

2. Include multi-sensory reinforcement materials, such as those described below.

•Cards on which numbers, letters, and words are written with Elmer's glue and covered with yarn, sand, salt, bird seed, small bits of tissue paper, dried beans, peas, macaroni, or sandpaper.

•Letter or word cards covered with acetate or slipped into an acetate window for students to trace.

•Manipulative devices such as those described in Chapter 5.

3. Develop manipulative activities such as these:

•Students use flannel or magnetic letters or numerals to form words or number sentences.

•Students form letters, words or numerals in shaving cream, sand, water, pudding, or finger paint.

•Students match letter, word, and/or number cards.

•Students write letters, words, sentences, paragraphs, or numerals on chalkboard and large sheets of newsprint.

4. Develop activities which are self-correcting so students can have immediate feedback.

5. Prepare very short, concise directions.

•Illustrate directions whenever possible

•Provide ample margins

•Number steps

•Prepare directions in "rebus" form, if appropriate.

6. Use similar directions and procedures for centers in various skill areas so that students can focus on center content without being confused by different directions and procedures. Preteach directional words.

7. Develop a reference chart for directional words. E.g.,

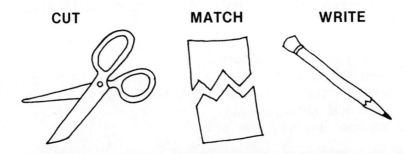

CUT   **MATCH**   **WRITE**

8. Review and discuss on a daily basis procedures for using centers, directions for using specific centers, and students' progress and problems in using centers.

9. Develop assignment and record keeping procedures for center use which are very simple. Use these procedures consistently.

10. Encourage students to use a center as many times as it appears to be helpful to them.

11. When using centers for the first time, begin with very simple center activities such as listening to records or tapes and making illustrations for projects or stories.

12. Use all centers in a teacher-directed setting before directing students to use them independently.

13. Consult with special education resource specialists and reading specialists regarding the skills that individual students need to have reinforced at the time when these students are receiving services from these specialists.

The Student With Specific Language Disabilities

Students with specific language disabilities may also have more generalized learning disabilities. These suggestions are applicable primarily to those students of average or above average intelligence who have difficulty with the printed symbols that stand for language.

Learning characteristics usually associated with the student with specific language disabilities include:

- average or above average ability to conceptualize, verbalize, and do abstract thinking
- general difficulty dealing with the symbols which represent language
- difficulty with auditory and visual sequencing
- difficulty with auditory and visual memory
- problems with directionality and organization
- difficulty with handwriting
- difficulty with spelling
- need for much structure and organization in learning experiences
- tendency to omit words and letters from writing, or skip words and sentences in reading
- persistent reversals in letters and words after Grade 2

Here's how to adapt centers for the student with specific language disabilities:

Planning

1. Coordinate centers with daily instructional activities as

closely as possible in order to provide immediate reinforcement of skills which have been presented.

2. Plan many centers around the same objective to provide students with intensive and extensive reinforcement opportunities to "overlearn" skills.

3. Plan centers which consist of tasks that can be completed in a relatively short period of time to keep student's attention focused on the current task and to give them a feeling of accomplishment and closure. Short activities with concrete, easily identifiable objectives and tasks help these students develop confidence in themselves as learners.

4. Plan several year-round centers to help students master very basic reading, writing, and spelling skills. Examples of such centers would include:

- "Read along" centers featuring stories which are appealing to students and tapes of those stories
- Spelling study centers
- Handwriting practice centers.

Developing and Using

1. Make center activities manipulative whenever possible in order to focus students' attentions on the task at hand, and to provide additional multi-sensory input for them.

2. Make center activities multi-sensory whenever possible by combining visual, auditory, and tactile-kinesthetic (touching, tracing) experiences.

3. Provide auditory reinforcement in center activities whenever appropriate.

- Use tape recorders, record players, and language masters to present directions and/or information.
- Make tapes (or have students make tapes) of content materials in social studies, science, etc.

4. Prepare materials and activities which can provide tactile-kinesthetic reinforcement for students.

a. Make letter, word, or phrase cards on which letters and words are written with Elmer's glue and covered with yarn, sand, salt, bird seed, small bits of tissue paper, dried beans, peas, macaroni, or sandpaper.

b. Develop center activities in which students make the items described above.

c. Prepare letter, word, or phrase cards which can be covered with acetate or slipped into acetate windows for students to trace.

d. Develop activities such as these for centers:
  - Students match letter, word, and/or number cards.
  - Students form words from letter cards, or number sentences from numeral cards.
  - Students use magnetic letters or numerals to form words or number sentences on a magnetic board.
  - Students use flannel letters or numerals to form words or number sentences on a flannel board.
  - Students type letters, words, sentences, or numerals.
  - Students write on transparencies.
  - Students form letters, words or numerals in shaving cream, sand, water, pudding or finger paint.

5. Make center directions as simple and uncluttered as possible.
  a. Provide ample margins
  b. Number steps
  c. Include illustrations and examples
  d. Prepare directions in "rebus" form when appropriate.

6. Use similar directions and procedures for centers in various skill areas so that students can focus on center content without being confused by different directions and procedures.

7. Develop center activities in which students take short dictations from taped content in any subject area, check their completed dictations against an answer key, and make needed corrections.

8. Avoid center activities which require an extensive amount of writing.

9. When students first begin to use centers, develop center activities which are simple enough both to enable students to complete the activities successfully and to become familiar with the procedures involved in using centers. In this way the frustration which may result from students having to learn *how* to use centers at the same time they are trying to complete unfamiliar or difficult center activities is minimized.

10. Use all centers with students as a teacher-directed activity in a group setting before you permit students to use the centers independently.

11. In teacher-directed, small group settings, work with students to develop a schedule to follow in using centers. Assist them to organize their time by listing in order the activities which they will do, and estimating the amount of

time they will need to accomplish those tasks. Encourage them to keep their lists with them, and to check off activities as they are completed.

12. Pre-teach directional words, and have students demonstrate in a teacher-directed setting what is meant by directional words such as cut, paste, color, match, find, circle, underline, draw, and trace.

13. Review general procedures for using centers on a daily basis.

14. Review directions for using specific centers on a daily basis.

15. Encourage students to use a center as many times as they appear to be helped by it.

16. Consult with special education resource specialists and reading specialists regarding the skills that individual students need to have reinforced at the time when these students are receiving services from these specialists.

The Gifted Student

Students may be gifted in many different areas. Not all gifted students are academically gifted. They may display their giftedness in such areas as the creative arts, athletics, leadership ability, and social interaction.

Learning characteristics usually associated with gifted students include:

- persistent curiosity
- creativity
- ability to abstract and conceptualize
- a questioning attitude
- a desire to know the "how and why" of things
- keen powers of observation
- interest in hobbies and making collections
- a sense of humor
- a broad background of information
- ability to note similarities and differences
- advanced vocabulary

Here's how to adapt centers for gifted students:

Planning

1. Use centers as a means to broaden and extend curriculum offerings for students by designing centers which include:

a. Topics which are not presented in regular classroom curriculum materials.

b. A more thorough, extensive coverage of topics which are presented in regular curriculum materials.

c.Content specifically related to students' special interests.

2. Plan some centers which focus on identified basic skill needs of gifted students (e.g., handwriting, note-taking).

3. Have gifted students become part of a planning committee to plan centers which could be appropriate for and appealing to them.

4. Plan to include center activities that are enjoyable and fun as well as challenging.

Developing and Using

1. Include center activities which require critical thinking (e.g., compare and contrast, evaluate according to criteria, solve problems, determine relationships, draw conclusions, determine fact and opinion).

2. Include center activities which enable students to develop many different or unique responses to questions or solutions to problems.

3. Prepare center activities in which gifted students create products (e.g., designing a game, designing a unique machine, writing a book, creating imaginary places and things).

4. Prepare activities which include analogies and tasks which call for classifying or categorizing.

5. Design activities which require independent or small group research.

6. Design activities which encourage children to make collections (e.g., jokes, mottoes, tall tales, proverbs, maps, rocks, insects, bottle caps).

7. Design center activities which include challenging word puzzles, number pattern puzzles, riddles, codes, and "brain teasers".

8. Design activities which require students to identify fallacies, absurdities, bias and/or propaganda.

9. Include center activities which are open-ended. Some examples of open-ended language arts center activities are listed below.

- Compile an annotated bibliography on a subject of your choice for your classmates.

- Create a "game" show for TV. Develop a theme for your show and write activities and questions which would be used on your show.

- Write a short play or musical comedy. Include song lyrics if it is to be a musical production. Design costumes and scenery. Develop an advertising campaign for your production.
- Prepare a TV critic's column based on TV shows you have seen recently.
- Discuss the positive and negative features of newspaper editorials, cartoons, and/or features.
- Write several unfinished stories and/or comic strips for classmates to complete.
- Prepare a brochure describing the grand opening of a new children's bookstore.

10. Help gifted students plan and use their time efficiently when they are working with center activities. Planning charts or schedules can assist them to manage their time.

11. Develop standards with gifted students which they can use to assess the work they do with centers. These standards can help them determine if their tasks are complete, if they are accurate, if they have followed directions, and if their work is neat and appropriately organized. It is important to develop these standards with students rather than for them.

12. Help students select center activities which meet their needs. Assist students to develop an independent strategy for evaluating the appropriateness of a center activity for their use. For example, gifted students might be guided first to read directions for each activity in a center, and then begin with the activity which seems to them to be most appropriate. As teachers help students select center activities, there may be occasions when they wish to indicate specific entrance and exit points for students.

13. Work with gifted students to develop and use an independent record keeping system on which they chart their progress and evaluate their performance with center activities.

14. Conduct brief discussion sessions with gifted students in which they evaluate their progress with centers and habits which they display in using centers.

15. Maintain an on-going "suggestion box" in which students can place their comments and recommendations for centers.

Here's How to Use Learning Centers with Intermediate Students with Reading Difficulties

Intermediate students with poor reading skills need a "second chance for success" in learning basic skills. Furthermore, they need opportunities to keep pace with their peers in learning current content presented in curriculum areas such as social studies and science. Many of these students need to develop independent work/study skills and a positive attitude toward themselves as learners.

Intermediate students with reading difficulties may be above average, average, or below average in ability. They may come from any socio-economic environment. They have a wide spectrum of strengths and needs. Many of them feel frustrated and negative about school experiences and about themselves as students. There are many different reasons why these students experience reading difficulties. Some reasons are listed below:

- They may have had a learning style unsuited for the method used in teaching them to read (e.g., little or no phonics instruction offered to a child who learns best through auditory channels).
- They may have emotional and/or social problems which have interfered with their progress.
- They may have needed more practice or reinforcement than they received at various stages in learning to read.
- They may have missed important steps in learning through lack of continuity in their instructional program. This lack of continuity may have been caused by absences, transferring to different schools, frequent changes to different basal reading series, mid-year teacher changes, or lack of interest and participation in learning experiences.
- They may have difficulty dealing with the symbols that represent language, specific language disabilities. (See Chapter 3.)

- They may have had poor instruction.
- They may be slow learners. (See Chapter 3, for specific suggestions.)
- They may have general learning disabilities.

Regardless of the causes of their reading problems, all of these students share a common need: the need for successful learning experiences.

Learning centers are an especially effective teaching tool to use with intermediate students with poor reading skills.

- Centers offer these students a "second chance for success" in learning and reinforcing important basic skills in reading, language arts, and mathematics.
- Centers offer an opportunity for these students to learn content material in curriculum areas such as social studies and science through the use of activities which do not require extensive amounts of reading or writing.
- Centers offer an opportunity for these students to develop effective and efficient work/study habits.
- Centers offer an opportunity for these students to develop a positive attitude toward learning and toward themselves as learners.
- Centers offer an opportunity for these students to develop decision making skills and independent work/study habits.

Centers can provide such opportunities to these students because they can be designed around students' interests and skill needs. Centers can incorporate materials which have been developed at a level of difficulty which guarantees success. In addition, centers can be quite different from materials which students have previously associated with frustration and failure.

The following considerations may be helpful in determining how to use centers with intermediate students who have poor reading skills:

- Develop some centers which have been specifically designed for these students. For example, these students usually need many centers that provide for the reinforcement of basic skills which they have missed.
- Include in some centers developed for general classroom use activities that all students might do, but which are especially appropriate for the intermediate student with poor reading skills. These activities might be ones which present information primarily through non-print materials

such as pictures, tapes, and filmstrips; activities which include several manipulative devices (see suggestions in Chapter 5), or activities requiring project development.

- Have students use some center activities developed for general classroom use but modify procedures for using them to increase the likelihood that intermediate students will use them successfully. For example:

Provide additional teacher direction in introducing these center activities to students.

Provide ample time for completion of the activities.

Have students work as problem solving teams to complete center activities.

Have students do particularly difficult activities as group, teacher-directed activities.

- Include among centers for general classroom use some centers designed to develop or extend students' interests (see Chapter 2). Centers which focus on hobbies, art projects, games, or independent reading can be used enthusiastically by all students.

If students have an especially difficult time completing center activities, consider these possibilities:

1. The center activities may require that students use skills which they have not yet developed. These skills might best be introduced through group teacher-directed activities, and later reinforced through centers.

2. Students may not understand directions for using the centers. Review center directions with students in a small group setting, and provide sufficient examples so students understand clearly the tasks to be accomplished.

3. Students may have difficulty working independently. Pair these students with peers who can assist them.

Here's How To Develop Centers for Intermediate Students With Reading Difficulties.

Select Themes Which Build Motivation And Enthusiasm

Centers should have themes or topics highly interesting to intermediate-level students. These students frequently demonstrate interest in, and enthusiasm for, topics such as

Sports   Bikes, motorcycles and cars
Wild animals   Space and space travel
Pets   Monsters
Rock music   Clothes
Food   Television
Mysteries - detective   The ocean
stories, ghost stories   Jokes, riddles, and cartoons
Computers and calculators Folklore and tall tales
Codes
Heros and heroines

Present Basic Skills Through High-Interest Content

Learning centers can provide an opportunity for intermediate students to practice very basic skills without embarrassment because the skills can be presented through appropriately sophisticated themes. The chart below offers some examples of basic skill development through high-interest themes and materials.

SKILL	MATERIAL
•Using phonic elements.	•Students circle all words beginning with, ending with, or containing a specific phonic element in the sports, entertainment, or classified section of the newspaper. •Students complete sports headlines, song titles, etc., by using words containing key phonic elements. (E.g., Redskins *beat* Colts.)
•Identifying words which follow a specific spelling or syllabication generalization, or words containing specific prefixes or suffixes.	•Students underline appropriate words in "balloons" of comic strips. •Students cut appropriate words from magazine ads for bikes, cars, foods, or ads of interest to them.

SKILL	MATERIALS
• Identifying a sequence of events.	• Students place scrambled directions for a commercial game, such as "Sorry" in order. • Students place in order scrambled sentences from a report of a local school athletic event.
• Identifying a main idea.	• Students match captions with newspaper photos. • Students match recipes with names of food dishes. • Students match pictured items with catalog descriptions of the items. • Students match popular song titles with lyrics.
• Interpreting abbreviations.	• Students interpret abbreviations from used car ads. • Students interpret abbreviations from bus, train, or plane schedules.
• Practicing handwriting skills.	• Students complete sample order forms. • Students copy materials to ditto masters for use by class members. • Students prepare transparencies for group or class use.
• Practicing basic computation skills.	• Students solve problems based upon grocery ads, used car ads, ads from store sales, menus.

SKILL	MATERIALS
	•Students play games, such as "Scrabble" or "Yatze" which involve basic computations to keep score.
•Locating information.	•Students use the TV schedule to answer questions such as the following: How many movies are on Channel A this week? On which station is the "Wildlife Jungle Land Special" being presented? Which show begins earlier, "The Guessing Game" or "Money Magic"? •Students use catalogs to locate and determine cost of specific items.

"Guarantee Success" By Developing Center Activities Consisting Of Short, Simple Tasks

Intermediate students experiencing reading difficulty often have behind them a history of incomplete assignments and partially accomplished tasks. So that learning centers do not provide simply one more opportunity for these students to become frustrated and to fail, centers should include several short, simple tasks rather than longer, more involved activities. Brief tasks which are based upon highly motivating themes and which require a minimum of reading and writing are most likely to be appropriate for these students. By working step-by-step to accomplish these types of short-term goals, students have a greater chance to reach a long term goal, and to reach it with confidence based upon tangible success.

It is important that students who have previously failed or have become discouraged with regular classroom materials experience immediate success with learning center activities so that they maintain an "I can do it" attitude toward the centers.

Provide Immediate Feedback Through Self-Correction

Many intermediate students with reading problems may have missed some essential steps in basic skills development. They need immediate feedback concerning the accuracy of their responses to tasks which involve learning or using these skills. Immediate feedback obtained through self-correction is especially beneficial for these students for these reasons:

- Correct responses are reinforced immediately, thereby strengthening that learning.
- Incorrect responses can be noted and changed immediately, thereby lessening the possibility of reinforcing incorrect association.
- Self-correction helps students avoid the embarrassment of making mistakes in front of their peers or teacher.

Develop Project-Based Center Activities

Center activities which involve the development of student-constructed projects can be highly motivating to intermediate students with reading problems.

Project construction encourages students to:

- follow directions accurately
- develop complete, tangible products
- demonstrate their learning strengths and skills to themselves, their teachers, and their peers
- focus their attention on a specific task

Several types of projects might be developed through center activities. Illustrations, charts and graphs, models, posters, costumes, collections, catalogues, ads, and dioramas are examples of projects students might develop as part of center activities. (See Chapter 2.)

Other types of projects might involve development of "media productions" such as tapes, transparencies, simple filmstrips, and photographs. To accomplish these activities, students must learn the content to be presented through the tapes, films and transparencies and also practice skills such as reading, speaking, and writing in order to develop a "quality product." Students can help establish standards for media productions which they are developing. Students might, for example, develop criteria similar to those mentioned below for their productions.

- •Speaking done on tapes should be clear.
- •Printing done on transparencies should be neat and evenly spaced.

Students might serve on a rotating evaluation committee to make suggestions for improving media productions. Those "productions" which are appropriate might be catalogued and added to the school's media center resources, or to a classroom media library.

In order that students complete project development activities successfully, the teacher can help them organize the activities into a series of specific tasks with estimated completion dates.

Use Audio-Visual Equipment In Centers

Intermediate students usually enjoy using audio-visual equipment, and derive a feeling of satisfaction and accomplishment from being able to operate the equipment successfully.

Many types of audio-visual equipment can be used effectively in centers. Some types of equipment appropriate for center use include:

- •Language masters
- •Typewriters
- •Overhead projectors
- •Filmstrip projectors
- •Opaque projectors
- •Cameras
- •Record players

These devices help students learn content without becoming discouraged by long or difficult reading and writing tasks. They also add variety to center activities. They encourage students to stay "on task" and focus their attention on the activities at hand.

Centers can be developed which instruct students how to use these devices effectively. Such centers not only teach students to operate audio-visual equipment, but also reinforce skills which involve following directions, identifying and following a "sequence" of steps, and explaining and describing procedures to peers.

Help Students To Use Their Time Efficiently

Intermediate students with reading problems need the opportunity to work through center activities at a pace which is appropriate for them. Some of these students may take more time than their peers to complete specific activities because many of their skills are less well mastered. However, these students usually need more than just additional time to use centers. They need to learn how to make efficient use of their work time rather than just being given more work time.

These suggestions may help students make more efficient use of their time:

1. To help students focus on the task at hand, have these students clearly define for themselves the task to be accomplished, and estimate how long they think it will take them to complete it. Have students do this with you in a teacher-directed setting.

2. To help students stay "on task", have them check off each task which is completed on a record sheet. You may want to have them indicate how long it took them to complete the task, and compare that time with their estimated time.

3. To minimize "off task" behavior, develop with students a strategy which they can use when they encounter a problem. For example:

    a. See the center helper for assistance.

    b. Note your problem on your record sheet or on a slip of paper. Put the materials away and select another activity. Discuss the problem with your teacher.

Develop An Independent Center Management System With Students

Intermediate students with poor reading skills frequently have learned poor study habits and have developed avoidance techniques to delay having to cope with group or individual tasks which embarrass or frustrate them.

Through working with students to develop an "independent center management system" (a system for center assignment, time scheduling, record keeping, and evaluation), they can learn to organize their time and direct themselves through center activities. Success in directing their own learning frequently helps students to develop respect for themselves as learners, and concurrently to improve their achievement.

Working with students to help them to develop an independent center management system deepens their sense of responsibility to the system and their involvement with it. In addition, it lessens the chance that students will avoid or resent it since they have helped to develop it. It is important to take time to teach students how to use the system, and discuss their progress on a very frequent, regularly scheduled basis.

Individual student progress folders are especially effective for use in a center management system for intermediate students. Individual folders help students avoid the embarrassment of comparisons which group record keeping/ assignment/evaluation devices sometimes create. Individual folders assist students to develop efficient work/study habits because they help students to plan and organize their work, and to assess their progress continually.

A student progress folder might contain:

1. A list of the center activities which were prescribed for him/her.

2. A record card upon which the student records center activities that he or she has completed. This card provides the student with an evaluation of his/her performance with center activities.

3. A schedule on which the student can plan his/her time.

4. Completed assignments for teacher evaluation and comment.

Chapter 5

Tips for Learning Center Construction

Many teachers who would like to use centers in their class-rooms are hesitant to do so because they feel they do not have sufficient time, materials, or assistance to construct centers. With so many demands on teachers' time and limitations on resources available for materials of instruction, it is necessary to use time and resources for center construction as efficiently as possible.

The suggestions in this chapter are designed to help you save time, effort, and expense when you are constructing centers. Included are ideas for

- making simple manipulative devices for centers
- adapting these manipulative devices to a variety of skills (Reference Chart)
- adjusting centers to classroom size (display, storage, and workspace)
- making efficient, economical, and creative classroom adaptations of published materials
- making center materials durable
- getting students involved with center construction.

Teachers sometimes feel they cannot make centers because they have little or no "artistic talent." The materials described on the following pages can be and have been constructed easily and successfully by numerous teachers and students.

You *can* do it! Here's how.

Here's How To Make Simple Manipulative Devices In Learning Center Activities

Students respond enthusiastically to manipulative devices which are used in center activities. Manipulative devices tend to keep students' attention focused on the task to be accomplished, provide variety in learning tasks, and make learning fun.

The section which follows describes a variety of simple teacher-developed manipulative devices that can be used in center activities.

These manipulative devices can be helpful to you in constructing centers in the ways listed below.

- They can be related to the interests of the students.
- They can be adapted to any curriculum area (See the skills chart.)
- They can be constructed from inexpensive, readily accessible materials.
- They can be made as durable as you desire.
- They can be adjusted in size to fit any display, work, and/or storage space.
- They can be adjusted to supplement any curriculum materials.
- Students can make them.
- Many types of published materials can be "recycled" by using them in these devices.
- Many types of everyday household materials (boxes, cans, scraps of cloth, etc.) can be utilized in constructing these devices.
- They take little time to construct.
- Most can be made self-correcting.

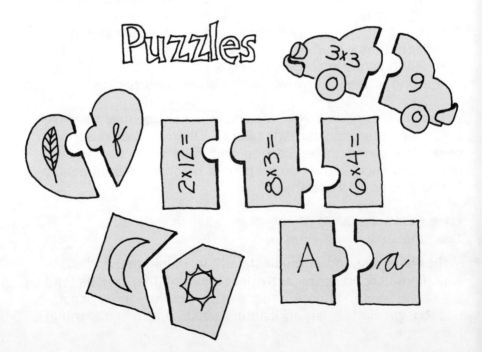

How To Make Puzzles

1. Select paper, tagboard, index cards, or cut-out shapes for the puzzles.
2. Draw a "zig-zagged" line to divide the puzzles.
3. Draw or write the items which are to appear on the puzzles.
4. Cut the pieces apart.

How To Use The Puzzles

Students match questions and answers, and check by determining if the puzzle pieces fit.

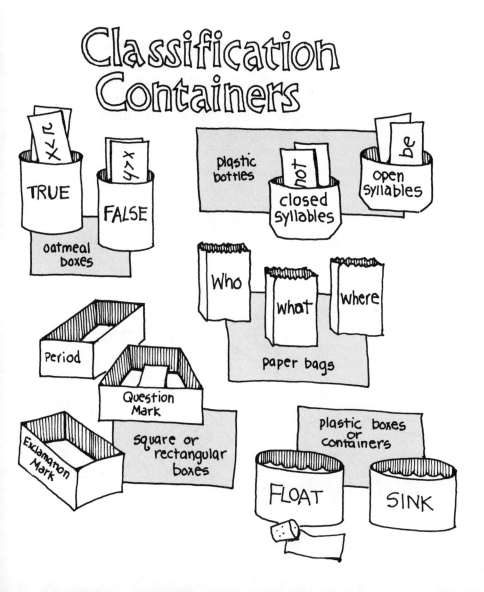

How To Make The Classification Containers

1. Select boxes, bags, or cans of appropriate size; e.g., plastic food containers, boxes, oatmeal boxes, coffee, food, or juice cans, or plastic bags, plastic bottles with top part removed, etc.

2. Cover with contact paper, construction paper, wallpaper, paint or magic marker, if desired.

3. Place appropriate labels on boxes.

4. Select, collect, or construct things to be categorized. Put answers on the back or make a separate key, if desired.

How To Use The Classification Containers

Students sort objects, pictures, words, problems, etc., into the appropriate containers. When all items are sorted, they check their work. Answers can be on the backs of the containers or on separate answer keys.

How To Make The Mushroom

1. Cut a "mushroom" shape from heavy paper.

2. Determine how many items are to be placed on the mushroom.

3. Using a hole punch, punch one hole around the top of the mushroom for each item to be included.

4. Write the items beside or under each hole.

5. Put the answers on the back so that they are directly behind the items on the front.

6. Laminate the mushroom or cover it with contact paper, if desired.

How To Use The Mushroom

Students work in pairs. One student holds the mushroom so that he or she sees the items on the front and his or her partner sees the answers on the back. The student holding the mushroom places a straw in one of the holes and gives the appropriate response. The partner then reads the answer as shown on the back.

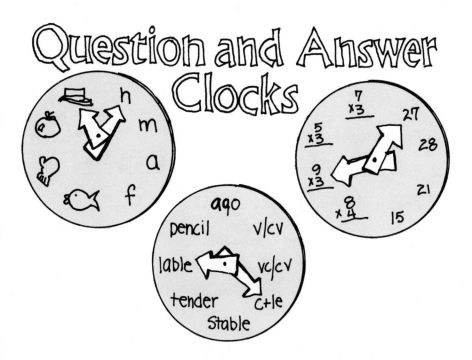

How To Make The Question And Answer Clock

1. Cut a circle from heavy paper, or use a plain paper plate.

2. Put questions on the left side of the circle, and answers on the right side.

3. Put an answer key on the back, if desired.

4. Attach two arrows or "hands" with a paper fastener.

How To Use The Question And Answer Clock

Students match questions with answers by placing one arrow on the question and the other on the answer. Then, they can check the answer from the key on the back of the clock.

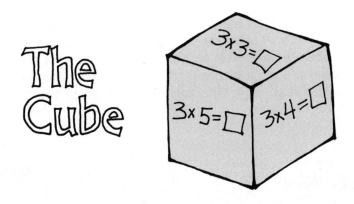

How To Make The Cube

1. Fold a sheet of paper in half.

2. Fold it in half again.

3. Fold it into thirds.

4. Open the paper and crease the folds up toward you.

5. Place small dots in the six squares indicated in the diagram.

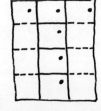

6. Write appropriate words, sentences, letters, numbers, etc., in the squares indicated by the dots.

7. Cut on the broken lines indicated in the diagram.

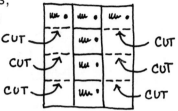

8. Shape the paper into a cube. Be certain the writing is on the outside faces of the cube.

9. Secure the sides with tape.

10. To make the cube more durable, laminate it or cover it with contact paper.

Other Ways To Make A Cube

1. Cut a quart or half gallon milk carton in half on three sides. Leave one side intact.

- Fold that side down as a top for the cube and secure it with tape.
- Write on the sides of the cube with magic marker or attach items with glue or tape.
- Cover the cube with plain contact paper.

2. Tape the lid of a small square box to the sides of the box. Cover with contact paper.

3. Use a wooden block.

4. Use a styrofoam block.

How To Use The Cube

Students roll the cube or toss it to a friend. They read what appears on top and complete the activity as the directions indicate. A separate answer key can be made available.

How To Make A Spinner

1. Cut a circle from heavy cardboard (any size). Two paper plates glued together also can be used.
2. Divide the circle into an appropriate number of sections.
3. Write or draw appropriate items in each section.
4. Put answers on the back of the circle if desired.
5. Make a small hole in the center of the circle.
6. Make an arrow out of a double thickness of cardboard. Glue the two pieces together.
7. Make a hole in the arrow that is *larger* than the hole in the circle.
8. Secure the arrow on the circle by using a paper fastener. Leave about ¼ inch of the paper fastener above the circle. Do not push the top of the paper fastener against the circle.
9. Fold the ends against the back of the circle. Cover them with masking tape.

How To Use The Spinner

Students simply spin the arrow. Students do whatever task is on the section where the arrow stops. They can check their work by looking on the back of the spinner.

Pocket Cards

Front of Pocket Card

3+3 = ☐
6

3:00

Back of Pocket Card

3:00

Tab Card

How To Make Pocket Cards

1. Fold a pocket in the bottom of a sheet of paper (any size).
2. Secure the sides with tape or staples.
3. Make a tab card to insert in the pocket.
4. Write the question or problem on the front of the pocket card above the pocket.
5. Write the answer on the back of the pocket card.
6. Write the answer on the tab card.

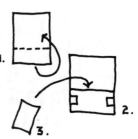

How To Use The Pocket Cards

Students read the item on the pocket card and select the tab card which goes with it. The tab card is placed in the pocket. The answer is written on the back of the pocket card for student self-correction.

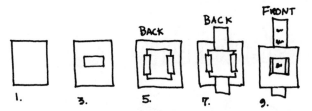

How To Make The Tachistoscope

1. Select a sheet of paper or picture for the tachistoscope.
2. Draw a rectangle on the paper that is a little larger than the longest word, phrase, picture, etc to be used in the tachistoscope.
3. Cut out the rectangle.
4. Cut a slip of paper that is larger than the window.
5. Cover the window with the slip of paper and tape its sides to the tachistoscope.
6. Cut a long narrow strip of paper to insert within the tachistoscope.
7. Insert the narrow strip of paper between the window and the paper covering it.
8. Pull the strip of paper down until its top is about ½ inch above the covering of the window.
9. Write an item (word, phrase, number, picture) on the part of the strip exposed by the window. Number each item to be written.
10. Pull the strip of paper up until the item disappears. Write another item on the part of the strip now exposed by the window.
11. Continue in this way until the strip is filled with items.
12. A separate answer key can be made if desired.

Note:

Tachistoscopes may be made in any size, shape, or design. Magazine pictures, children's drawings, geometric shapes, newspaper headlines and book jackets are examples of things that may be used for a tachistoscope base.

How To Use The Tachistoscope

Students insert a strip in the tachistoscope. They pull the strip up and study what is exposed by the window. For example, they read the word and give an opposite or read the number sentence and give an answer. They complete the activity as indicated by the directions and use the answer key.

Matching Cards

How To Make Matching Cards

1. Select durable paper and cut cards to desired size (or use index cards, computer cards, oak-tag strips, old playing cards).
2. Draw, write, or glue items on the cards.
3. Laminate or cover with clear contact paper, if desired.
4. Place answers on the back or, if desired, make a separate answer key.

How To Use Matching Cards

Students match questions with answers and check their work. Matching cards may also be used for concentration games.

Picture Puzzles

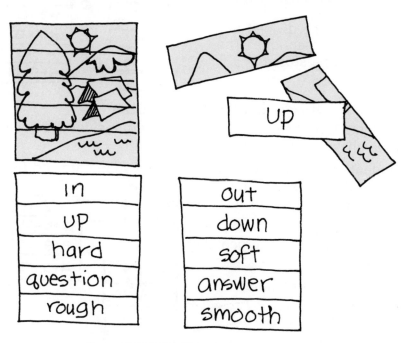

in	out
up	down
hard	soft
question	answer
rough	smooth

How To Make The Picture Puzzle

1. Divide two sheets of heavy paper into the same number of equal-sized sections. **Q.** **A.**

2. Write questions in the sections of one sheet and their answers in the corresponding sections of the second sheet.

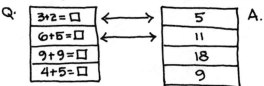

Q.
3+2 = ☐	5
6+5 = ☐	11
9+9 = ☐	18
4+5 = ☐	9

A.

3. Turn the answer sheet over and mount a picture on the back of it.

4. Cut along the lines which divide the answer sheet into sections. Keep the question sheet intact.

The sheet can be divided into any number of sections. The puzzle might be stored in a file folder.

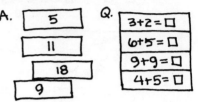

How To Use The Picture Puzzle

1. Students turn the strips so that the picture sides are down and the answers are facing them.

2. Students read the questions on the question card and find the strip which answers the question. This strip is placed on top of the question.

3. When all strips have been placed on the question card, each is turned over to reveal the picture.

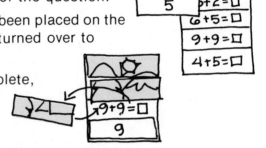

4. If the picture is complete, the task has been accomplished accurately.

Banks

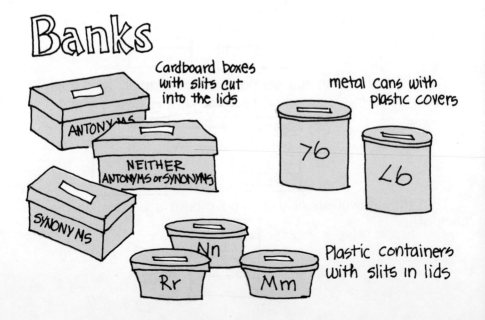

Cardboard boxes with slits cut into the lids

ANTONYMS

NEITHER ANTONYMS or SYNONYMS

SYNONYMS

metal cans with plastic covers

Plastic containers with slits in lids

How To Make Banks

1. Select an appropriate number of cardboard or plastic containers with covers.

2. Cut slits in the covers. The slits should be a little larger than the largest items to be placed in the banks.

3. Decorate the containers with pictures, decals, contact paper, or magic markers, if desired.

4. Label the containers.

5. Prepare "coins" to be used in banks by mounting each item on a circle of heavy paper or tagboard. Put answers on the backs of these "coins".

6. Cover with clear contact paper, if desired.

How To Use The Banks

Students take "coins" from a large container and sort them into appropriate "banks". After all coins are sorted, students check their work by looking at the answers on the backs of the coins.

Game Boards

How To Make Game Boards

1. Select the type of game board you prefer. Use materials for the board such as:

file folders
paper towels
construction paper or tagboard

long, flat cardboard box
old game board
cloth

2. Design the game board you want to construct. Simple game boards can be made by drawing a path, dividing the "path" into sections, and then numbering the sections or writing items in them.

3. Design and construct a set of items or activity cards if items or questions are not written directly on the game board.

4. Make the game board using your design as a model.

5. Make or select appropriate playing pieces. Playing pieces can be made in this manner: (1) Fold a small piece of construction paper in half. (2) With the fold at the top draw a design on both sides of the paper. (3) Cut around the design. Do not cut on the fold.

6. Make an answer key for the game.

7. If desired, laminate or use contact paper for any items made from paper.

8. If needed, make a spinner or cube to indicate number of spaces to be moved or type of task to be accomplished.

9. More elaborate game boards can be made by using two separate pieces of very heavy cardboard, covering them with contact paper, and joining and binding them with heavy plastic tape.

How To Use The Game Boards

Make simple rules such as these for the games:

1. Get a partner or form teams.
2. Draw a card. Do what the card tells you to do.

3. Check your answer.
4. If you are right, move your playing piece the number of spaces indicated on the card.

or

1. Get a partner.
2. Spin the spinner (or roll the cube).
3. Move your playing piece the number of spaces indicated.
4. Do what the directions on the game board tell you to do.
5. Check your work.

Reference Chart Of Skills Which Can Be Reinforced Through Use Of Manipulative Devices

READING

Vocabulary
• match words and definitions
• read words, use them in sentences
• match synonyms, antonyms, homonyms

Word Attack
• match pictures with letters (consonants, clusters, vowels) representing beginning, medial, or final sounds
• match words with contractions
• identify words containing prefixes and suffixes
• match words with compound words
• match generalizations with examples of generalizations
• read sentences and fill in missing words using phonics and context clues

Comprehension
• match questions and answers
• place events in sequence
• match picture, paragraph, or story with title
• complete analogies
• match statements of cause and effect

LANGUAGE

Language Arts
• identify or practice letter names and forms

- match capital and lowercase letters
- match manuscript and cursive forms

Language Usage
- select correct forms of words
- select correct tenses of words
- identify correct capitalization
- identify correct punctuation
- match spelling generalizations with spelling words

Literature
- match authors and titles
- match characters with authors, or titles
- describe story or character

Creative Writing
- select a title for a story

MATHEMATICS

Numerals and Sets
- match sets with numeral or word or set with same number of objects
- match number names with numerals

Computation
- complete number sentences
- match problem with answer
- match word problem with process needed to solve it

Fractions
- match fractional parts with fractions
- match equivalent fractions

Measurement
- match quantity to measure
- give equivalent measures

Time
- match clock face to time indicated

Geometry
- match geometric shapes with names or descriptions

Money
- match change with stated amount of money

Metric
- match metric words to the appropriate symbols
- match metric words or symbols to items measured in that unit
- match metric equivalents

SOCIAL STUDIES

Geography
- match cities or capitals with states or countries
- match mountains, rivers, etc with states or countries
- match maps with place names

History
- describe places, people, events of historical significance
- match names of famous persons, places, or events with descriptions of them
- place events on a time line
- match questions and answers
- match pictures to names

Current Events
- describe persons or events in the news

SCIENCE

- match animals to names
- classify items and information
- match questions and answers
- give descriptions or characteristics of processes, phenomena, or things
- match statements to true or false

MUSIC

- match notes and names
- match pictured instruments and their names
- match composers and compositions

•identify composer, instrument, composition
•describe composer, instrument, composition

CAREER AWARENESS

•match occupation to job cluster
•match job to supporting occupations
•match tools or apparel to occupation

Here's How To Adjust Centers To Classroom Size

Centers can be used effectively in classrooms with very limited storage, display, and workspace as well as in large, open classrooms or wings. Although the content and activities included in centers for these two different types of classrooms can be the same, the way the centers are packaged and displayed will vary according to the amount of space available.

Teachers who have small classrooms usually prefer to use compact centers which require very little storage, display, and workspace. Teachers who have larger classrooms may wish to use a combination of compact centers and centers which are displayed over a large area. The following suggestions may help you adjust your centers to the space you have available in your classroom.

Developing Compact Centers

Compact centers are those which are developed and packaged in a manner which requires little display, storage, and work space. These centers provide much flexibility in center use.

•They can be used in any classroom, large or small.
•They can be moved (carried) conveniently from one classroom to another.
•They can be stored easily for later use.
•They can be taken to students' desks or assigned work areas.
•They can be displayed in a minimum of space.
•They can be sent to the child who is recuperating at home.

Examples of Compact Centers

Folders

Pocket Folders

Activities inserted in acetate sheets

Envelopes

Boxes

Cans

Plastic Bags

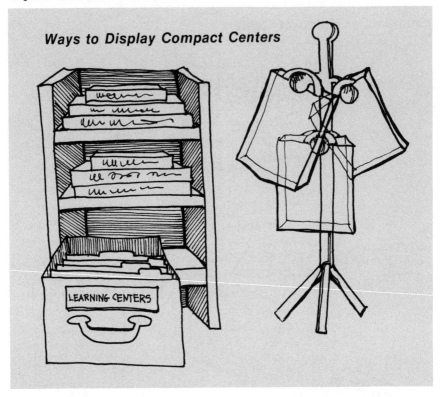

Ways to Display Compact Centers

LEARNING CENTERS

Developing Large Centers

Large centers are those which are developed and packaged in a manner which requires extensive display and workspace. These centers are especially appropriate for large classrooms and wings.

- Students can complete center activities at the center display area.

- Several students can work at the center display area simultaneously.

- The centers add attractiveness and appeal to the classroom setting.

- Several center work areas can be established in the classroom.

- Activities can be included in centers which require use of a large work area.

Examples of Centers on a Large Display Area

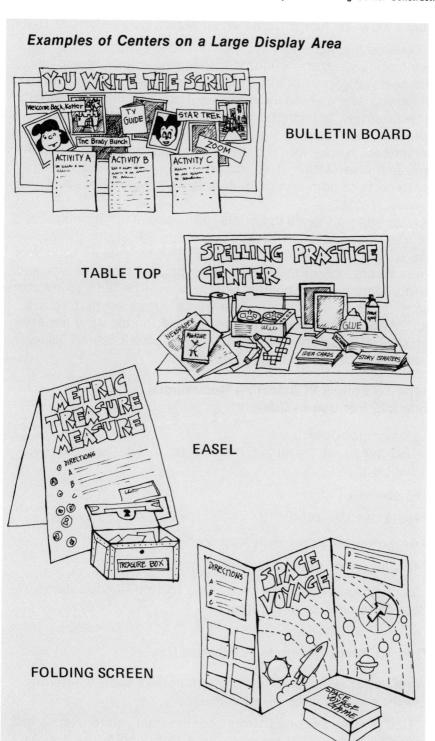

BULLETIN BOARD

TABLE TOP

EASEL

FOLDING SCREEN

Here's How To Adapt Commercial Materials For Center Use

Commercial materials such as textbooks, workbooks, spirit duplicating masters, children's magazines and newspapers, and parts of games or kits can help you save time and money when you are making learning centers. Teachers frequently receive single examination copies of new educational textbooks or workbooks from publishers or district resource personnel. In addition, old and/or damaged materials usually are readily available. It is important to select and use only those parts of commercial materials which are appropriate for specific centers.

Adapting published materials from several different sources for use in centers can help you provide variety in the activities which you prepare for centers. Because each source is likely to present different activities for the development and reinforcement of a specific skill, you will be able to design many types of center activities which focus on that specific skill. Although most of the time you will be locating material for use in specific centers, you may also wish to keep a general file of materials for future use.

Steps To Follow In Selecting Commercial Materials For Use In Centers

1. List center objectives.
2. List types of materials needed to make the center activities; e.g.,

- pictures of animals,
- sets of math problems,
- information about early explorers,
- examples of different kinds of graphs.

3. Look through available materials to find needed items to adapt for inclusion in centers.

Ways To Adapt Materials For Center Use

The purpose for selecting these materials should determine how they are adapted for center use.

1. Use entire sections from commercial materials; e.g., stories from old basal readers, units from content textbooks, or articles from children's magazines.

These sections can be bound in notebooks or folders or stapled into individual booklets.

2. Use intact pages from materials such as workbooks or student newspapers. These pages can be laminated, covered with clear contact paper, or slipped into acetate covers.

3. Use specific activities cut from pages in commercial materials.

These activities can be mounted on sturdy paper and laminated, covered with acetate or contact paper, or attached to some of the manipulative devices described.

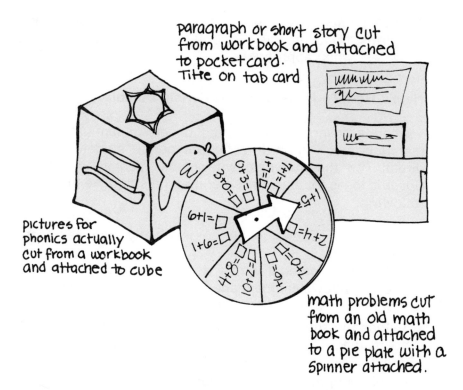

paragraph or short story cut from workbook and attached to pocket card. Title on tab card

pictures for phonics actually cut from a workbook and attached to cube

math problems cut from an old math book and attached to a pie plate with a spinner attached.

Prepare suitable directions and answer keys for these materials.

4. Use ideas and content from commercial materials as a reference in developing center activities.

5. Use commercially prepared word cards, letter cards, or picture cards in center activities when appropriate.

6. Make a learning center from commercial materials by following steps such as these:

a. Select from the total set of materials those to be used in the center.
b. Place the materials into sets according to level of difficulty, with each set becoming one activity in a multi-level center.
c. Add additional activities and materials, if needed.
d. Make the activities self-correcting through use of a separate key or by placing answers on the backs of the materials.
e. Prepare directions for the activities.
f. Select a packaging format (box, folder, envelope).

7. Use commercially prepared materials such as tapes, slides, filmstrips, transparencies, records, and photographs in center activities, when appropriate.

Here's How To Make Center Materials Durable

Acetate covers, clear contact paper, or lamination make materials much more durable, and permit students to write directly on the materials with grease pencils or crayons. Specific ideas for making center materials durable include the following:

1. Inserting material within commercially produced acetate covers.
2. Inserting material within acetate windows of any size. These windows can be made by binding two acetate sheets together on three sides with masking tape.
3. Inserting materials under the acetate cover of a study board made by stapling a sheet of acetate to a slightly larger sheet of heavy cardboard.
4. Covering materials with clear contact paper.
5. Laminating materials.

NOTE:

1. Clear contact paper usually can be purchased at hardware and department stores.
2. Acetate can be purchased from art supply stores.
3. Used x-ray film secured from hospitals or doctors offices can be substituted for the acetate.

Here's How To Get Students Involved with Center Construction

Getting students involved with center construction can provide important learning experiences for them. As students help to construct center materials they receive reinforcement with many of the skills presented in the center. For example, students who find words in newspaper headlines to use in a center on synonyms reinforce their own skills in identifying synonyms as they locate words for the center. Assisting with center construction encourages students to work neatly and accurately, and to follow directions carefully in order to make center materials which their peers can use. Students develop a feeling of responsibility toward the maintenance of centers when they have helped to construct them. Many teachers feel that when students have a part in planning and developing centers, the students use center activities with more interest, enthusiasm, and commitment than most other classroom materials. In addition, the teacher, in getting students involved with center construction, has more time available for other types of planning.

Here are suggestions for ways in which students can become involved in center construction:

1. Form a planning committee* of students to offer suggestions for center activities and themes to use with centers.

2. Form a center evaluation team* to examine materials students have made to determine if they meet standards for use in centers. These standards should be developed by students through teacher-student discussions.

3. Have students look through newspapers, magazines, and old workbooks to locate specific items to use in centers. For example, students might find pictures, words, paragraphs, problems, diagrams, letters, cartoons, etc. These items could be placed in a materials file or box until needed.

4. Have students cut out and mount items to be used in centers.

5. Have students make some of the simple manipulative devices in Chapter 5 for use in centers. Demonstrate to a few students how to make these devices, and have them teach their peers to construct them.

6. Have students write directions for centers.

7. Have students help to make centers attractive by drawing or locating pictures, making letters, painting or covering containers with contact paper.

8. Have students work on center maintenance committees to repair and replace damaged center materials. See the "Fix It" Center on page 50.

*Committees and teams should include students with various levels of ability and various interests. Membership should be on a rotating basis.

Index

Notes

Notes

Notes